HICKORY THROUGH THE HARDIN LENS 80 YEARS OF PHOTOGRAPHY

RICHARD ELLER

HICKORY THROUGH THE HARDIN LENS 80 YEARS OF PHOTOGRAPHY

RICHARD ELLER

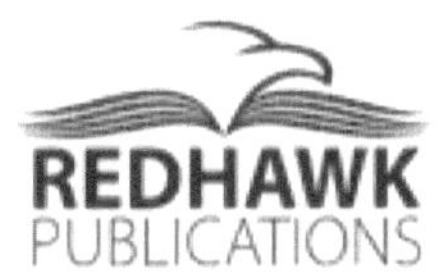

Hickory Through The Hardin Lens 80 Years Of Photography

ISBN: 979-8-89933-008-7 (Paperback)

Library of Congress Control Number: Applied For

Book design: Erin Mann
Cover design: Erin Mann

Printed in the United States of America.

First printing 2025

Redhawk Publications
The Catawba Valley Community College Press
2550 Hwy 70 SE
Hickory NC 28602
https://redhawkpublications.com

CONTENTS

CHAPTER 1

THE BEGINNING

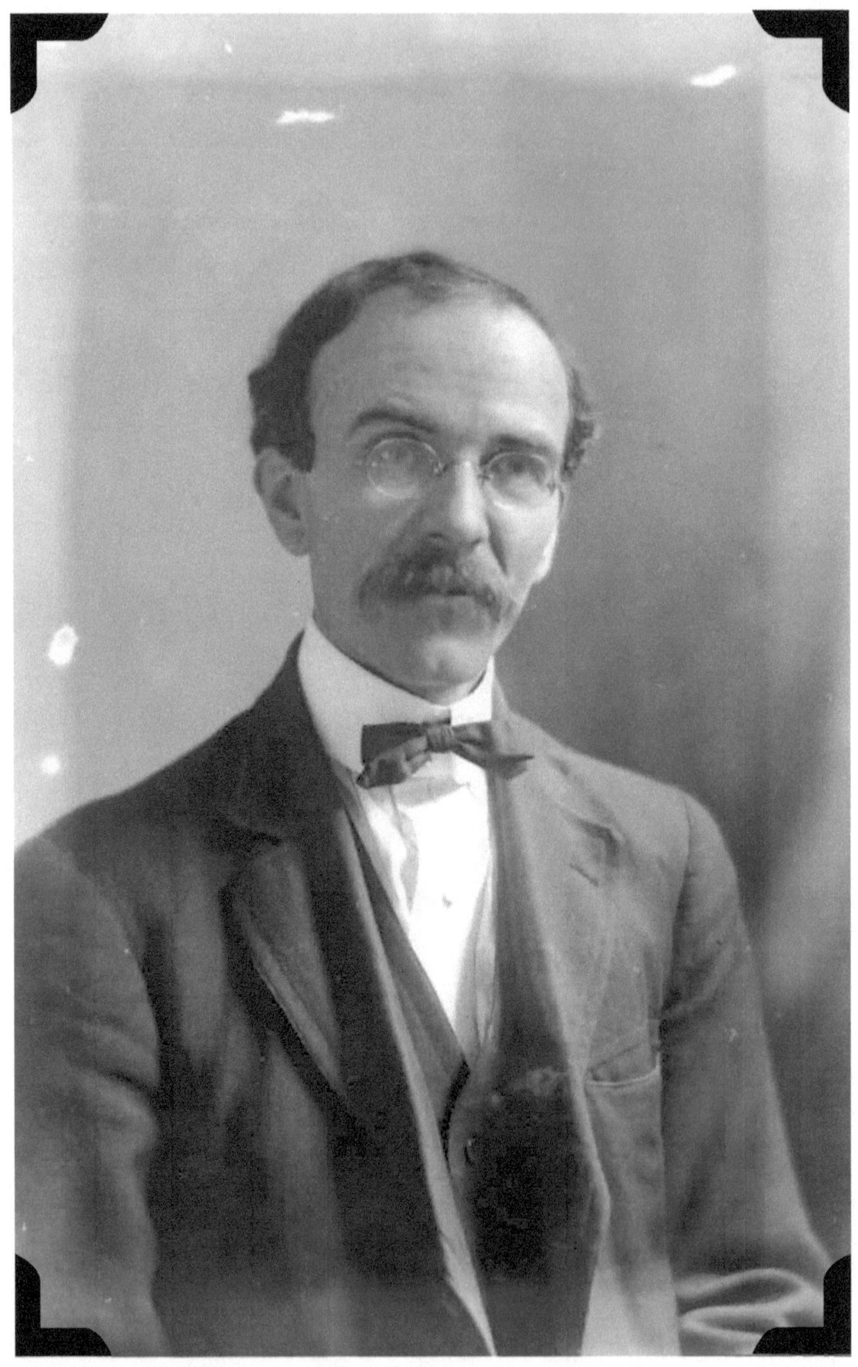

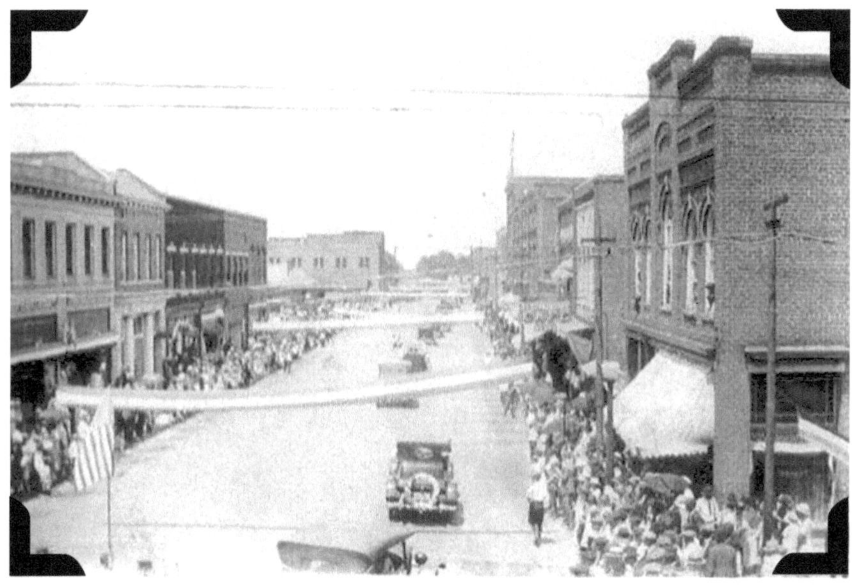

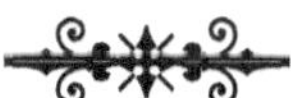

Charles McBurney Hardin arrived in Hickory in July of 1900, with his new bride and the tools of his trade, a camera. He was not the first photographer to set up shop in town, but he would prove to be the most enduring. Not long after he began Hardin Studios, C.M. reportedly bought the equipment of another lensman and worked out of their old studio, on the second floor of the original Woolworth building, located on the western end of Union Square.

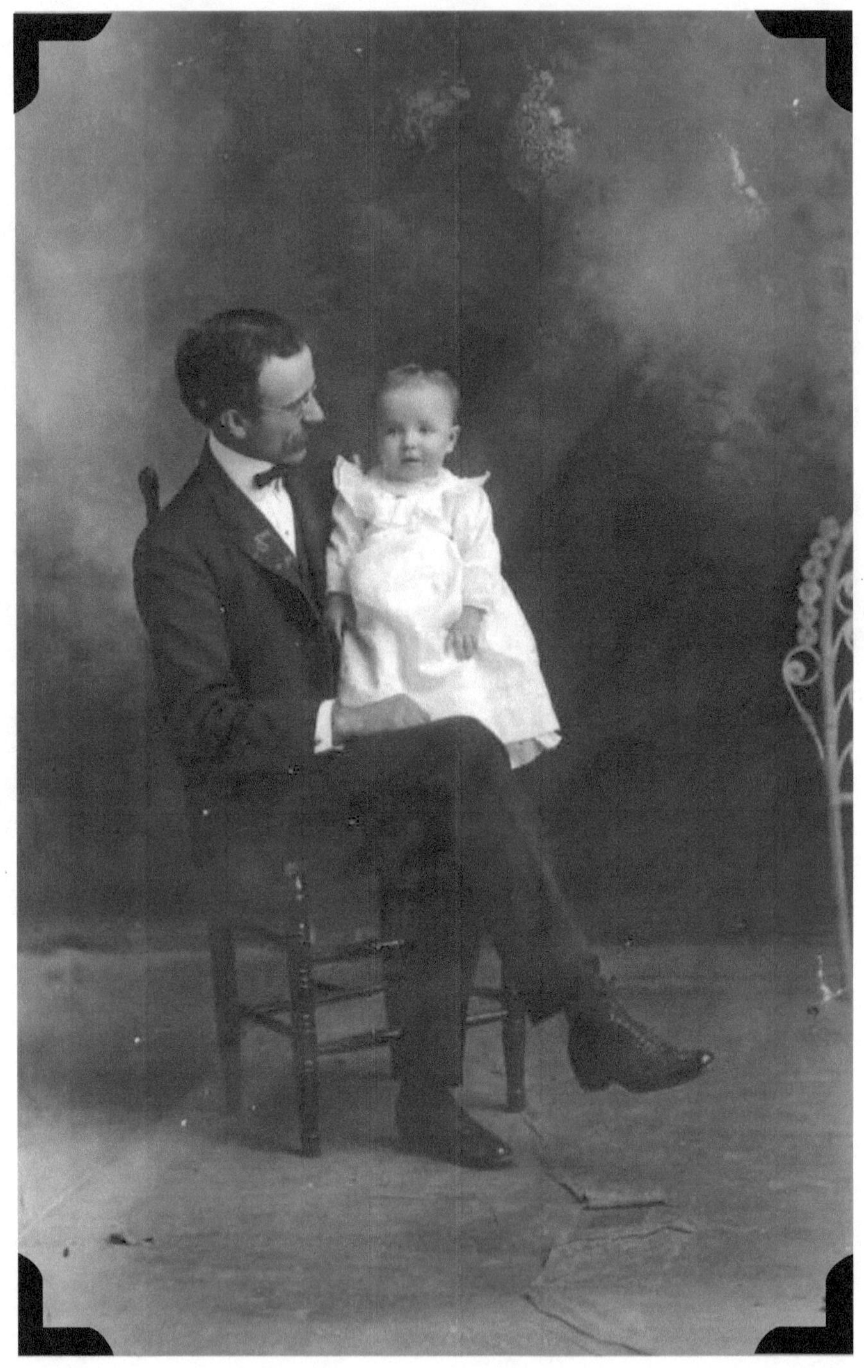

Within two years of settling down in Hickory, C.M. became a father. As he gazed on his infant daughter, he might not have realized that in his arms, he is holding his successor. Kathryn, after learning the trade from her father, would one day take over Hardin Studio. Their relationship was close, as the whole family spent many days together building the business. When she was born, the local paper took note, writing "Mr. C.M. Hardin is all smiles these days, owing to the arrival of a fine daughter at his home on July 31st (1902)."

Initially, he intended to guide his daughter into a career in music. She learned piano and was a gifted player. She may have been the reason that, for a while, Hardin Studio was an authorized piano dealer. "We handle pianos learning an international reputation and selling at a medium price," he told customers, "it will pay you to investigate before buying. Piano Display - - - Hardin's Studio." At first he represented "five leading piano factories in the country," before settling in as authorized dealer for Mehlin Pianos. Knabe-Crystola record players were also sold.

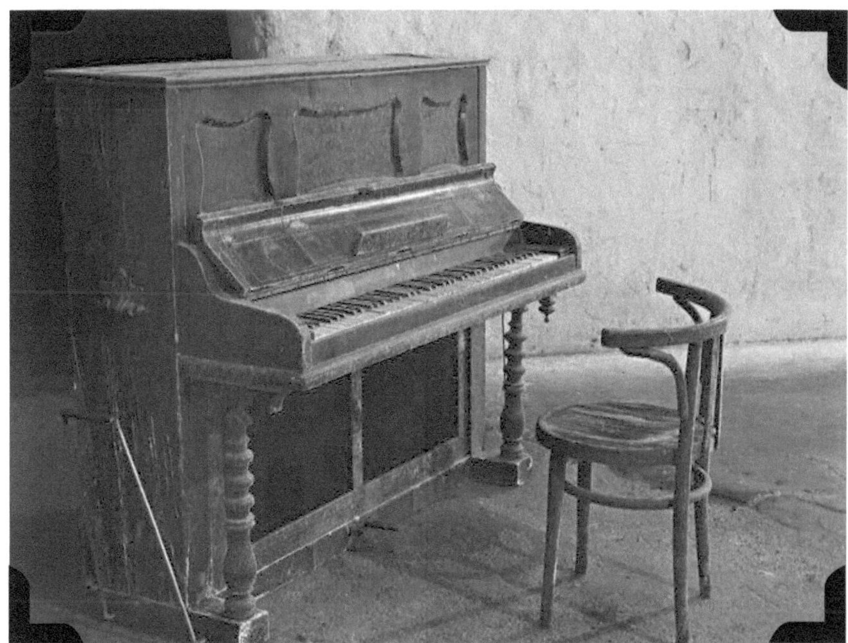

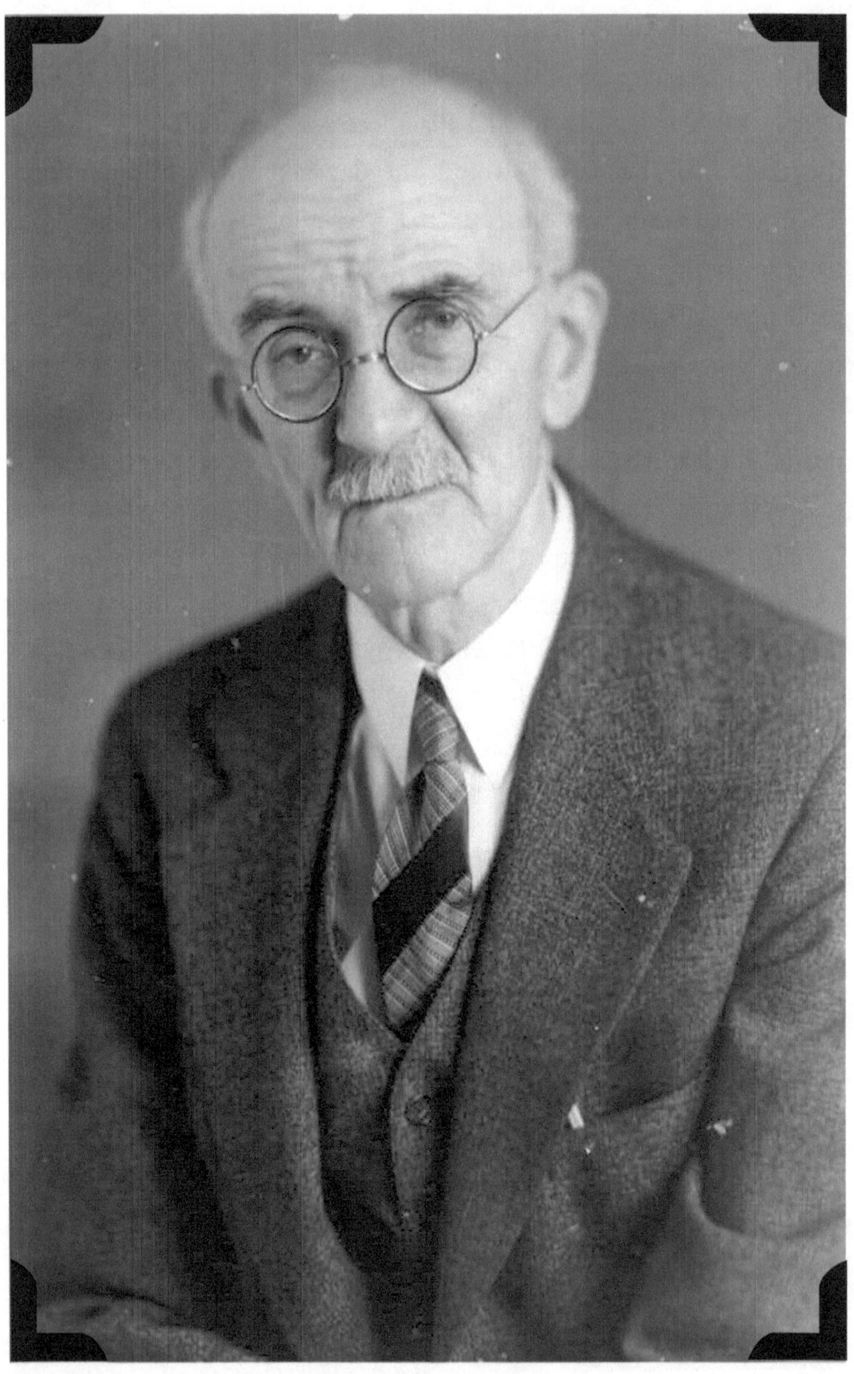

For forty years, C.M. Hardin served as a primary outlet for professional Hickory photography. This image, perhaps taken by his daughter, bookends his career. He died two years later. At that point, Kathryn was well positioned to take over the family business and become the city's premier portraitist for the next 40 years.

As a young man, C.M. chose to follow an interest in picture taking. The image (left) of the Whitener family was typical of the kinds of subjects C.M. encountered as an itinerant photographer. He rambled throughout the southeast looking for folks ready to have their images preserved for future generations. In his travels, C.M. veered from family reunions to capture this impromptu shot (below) of what might be entitled 'milking time.'

Given the technology of the era, making the effort to set up his camera to capture a moment like this, especially if no one was paying for the sitting, was time consuming. Yet something moved him to compose this shot for posterity.

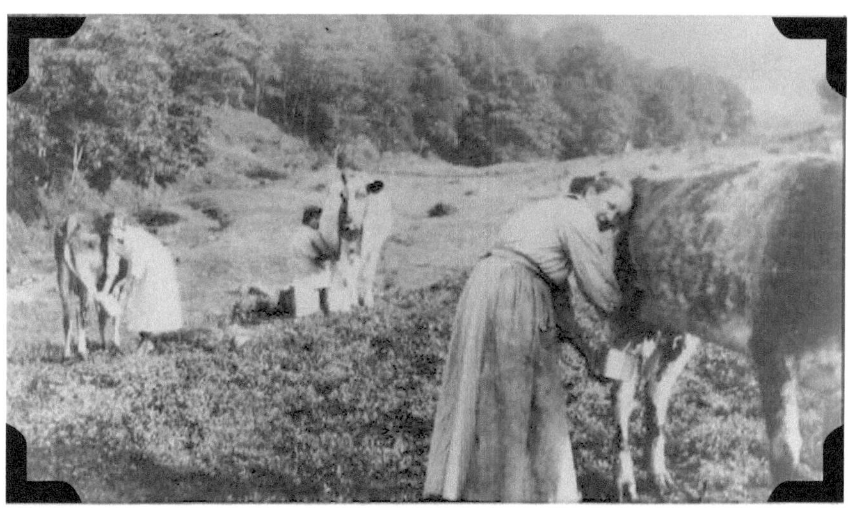

"A traveling photographer could pitch his tent in a neighborhood and take pictures for a month," C.M. once observed, "so eager were people for a likeness of themselves and families." To many in a clan, he brought a miracle in a box. For years after he had settled in Hickory, he traveled to many family reunions to document multiple generations in one sitting.

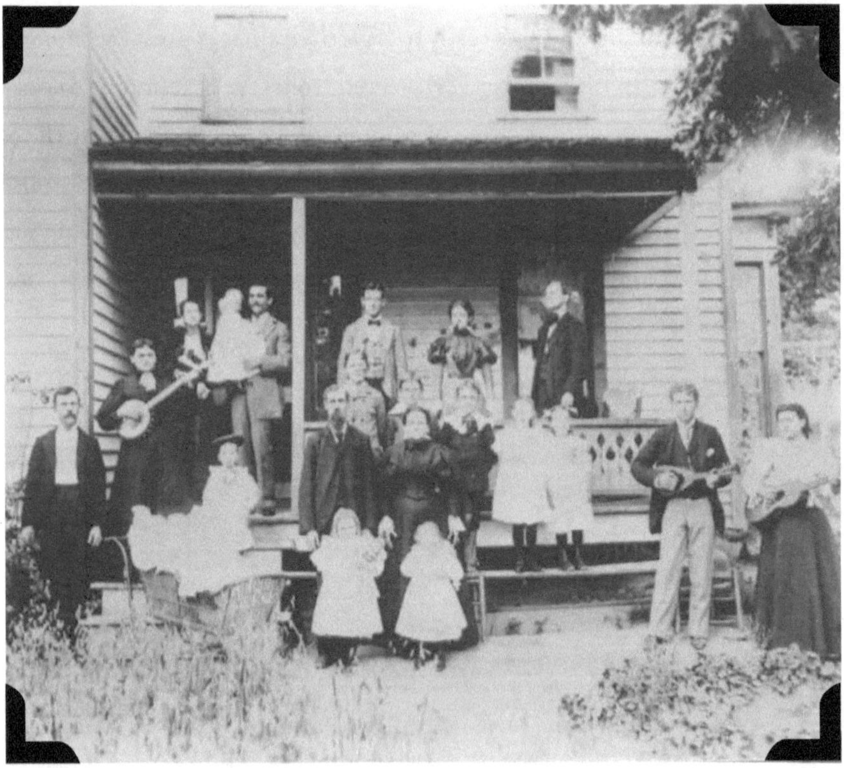

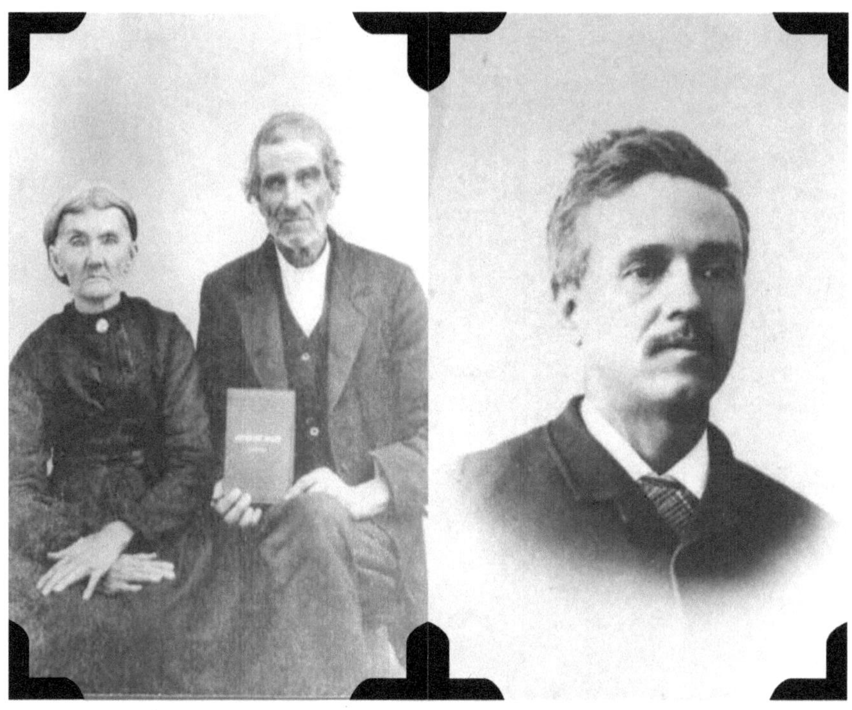

Pictured above left are C.M.'s paternal grandparents, Adley and Sarah Hardin. Both were born in North Carolina, he around 1808, she in 1815. Their son, Samuel Wright Hardin (right), born in 1842, served in the Civil War as a quartermaster sergeant for the 3rd North Carolina Mounted Infantry, a group of mountain unionists who fought against the Confederacy. Samuel returned to East Tennessee after the war, marrying Tempa Salina Mouke (Mauk) and started a family.

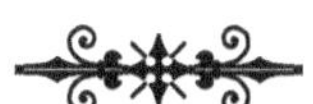

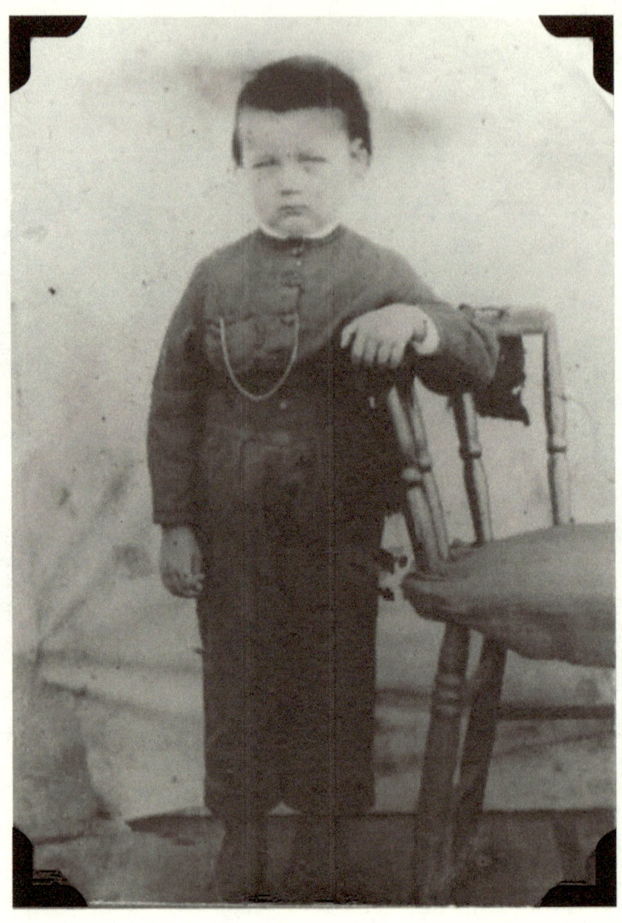

His firstborn came in 1868, was Charles McBurney Hardin, pictured above at an early age. The fact that so many images of the Hardins were taken suggests that the family prized photography as important family keepsakes. That fascination would spur C.M. into the profession, instead of the family tradition of farming. A likeness of Polly A. Mouke, C.M.'s maternal grandmother (right) suggests his love for photography came from both sides of the family.

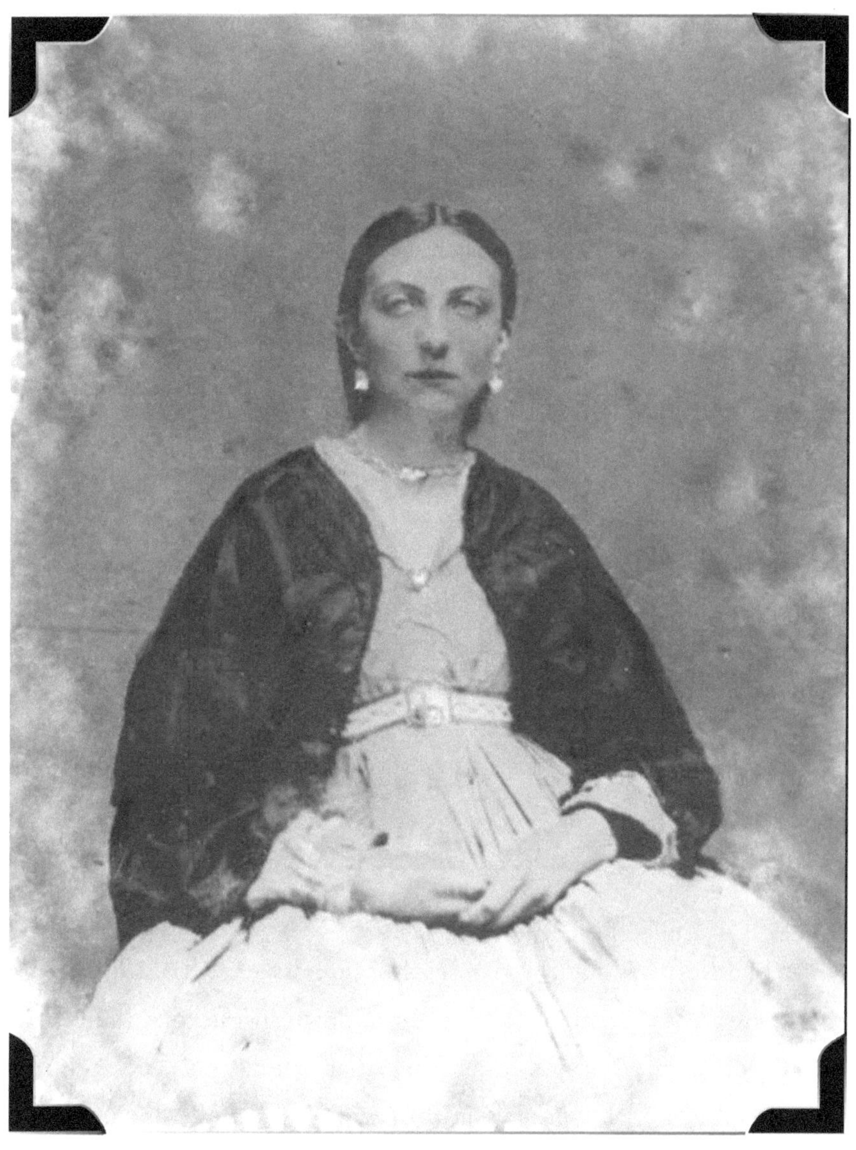

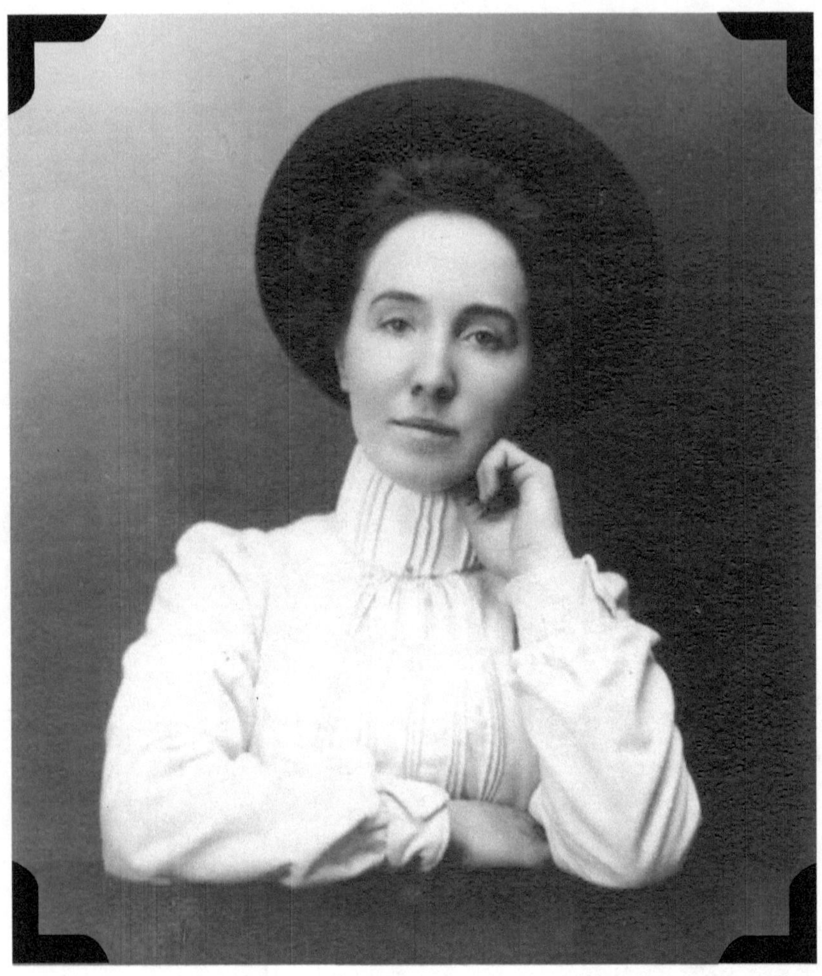

Immediately before coming to Hickory, C.M. married Leona Sykes Hardin. The couple wed in Bristol, Tennessee in April 1900 before their trek across the mountains to settle down in Hickory. Numerous images of Leona survive, indicating that she was C.M.'s primary photographic model, especially in the early days. Leona was snapped in a number of outfits, which also provide evidence of turn-of-the-century fashions.

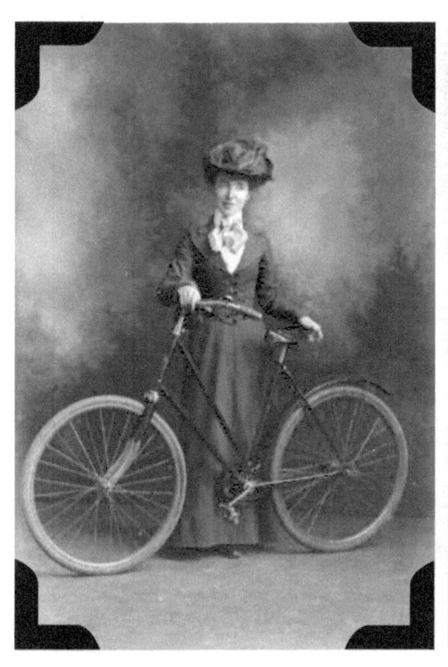
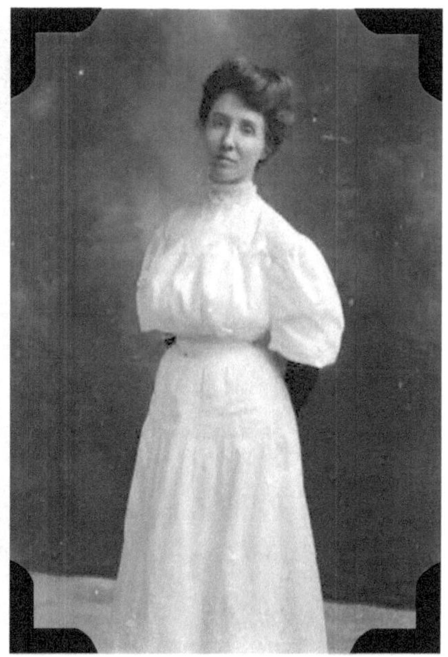

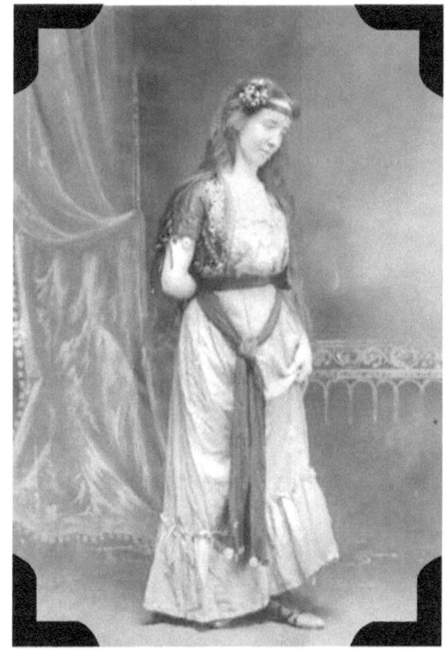
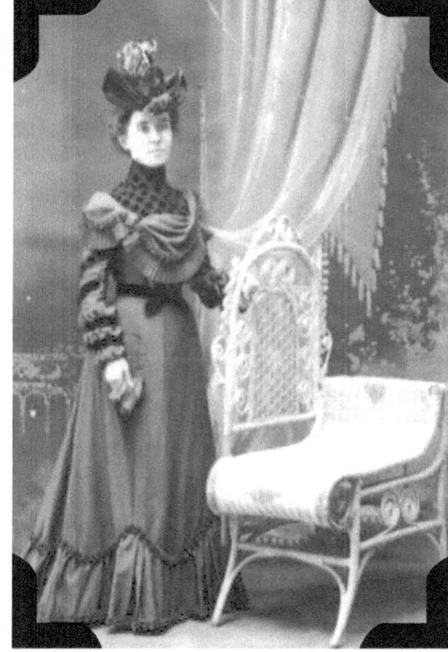

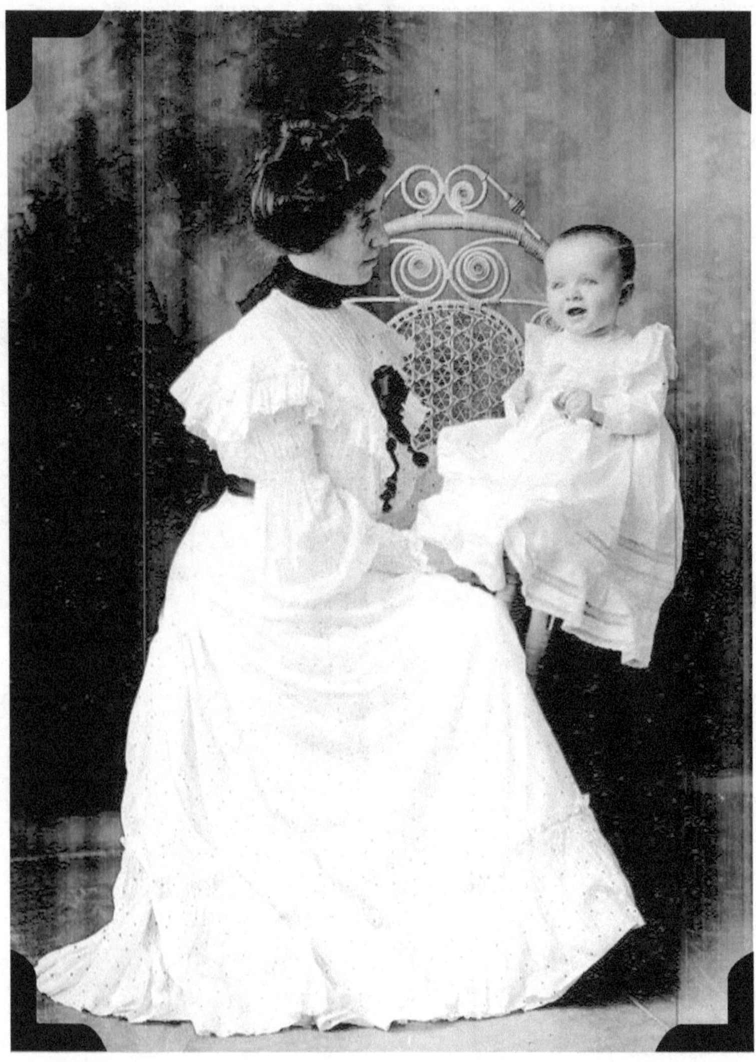

C.M. Hardin's other model of choice was his daughter, Kathryn. With and without her mother, Kathryn Hardin may have been the most photographed child in Hickory. From infancy through young adulthood, Kathryn was summoned into the studio regularly. The images show a girl growing up before our very eyes.

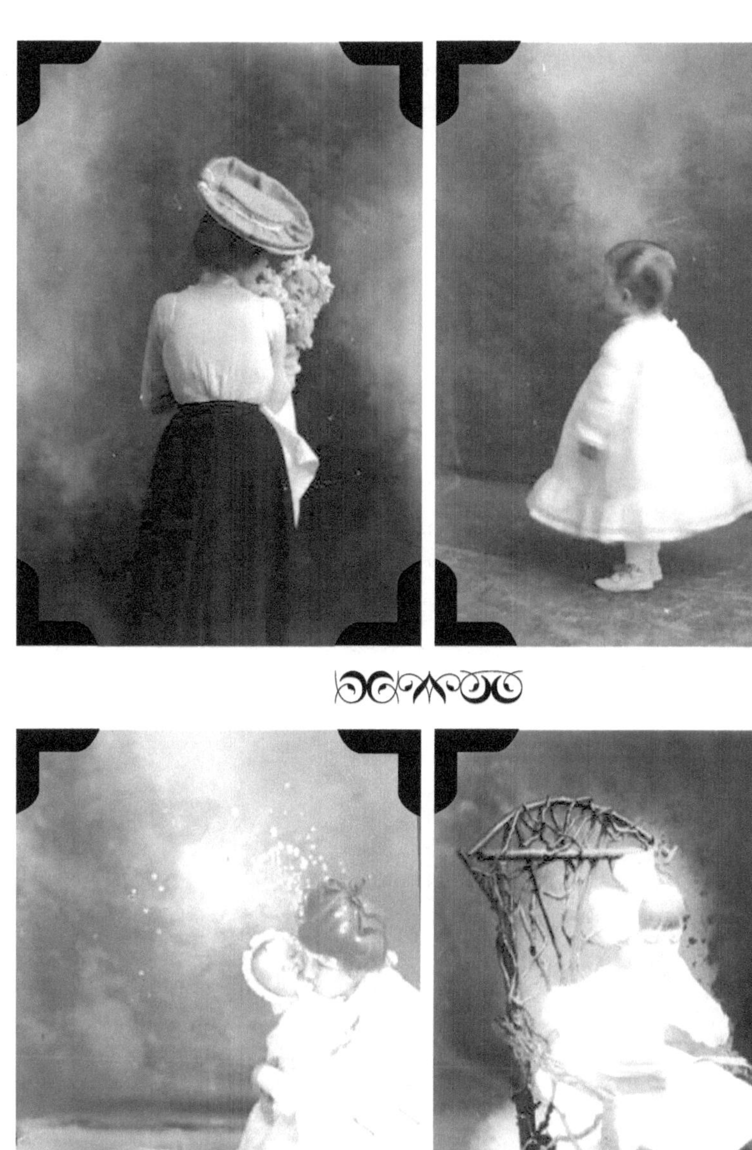

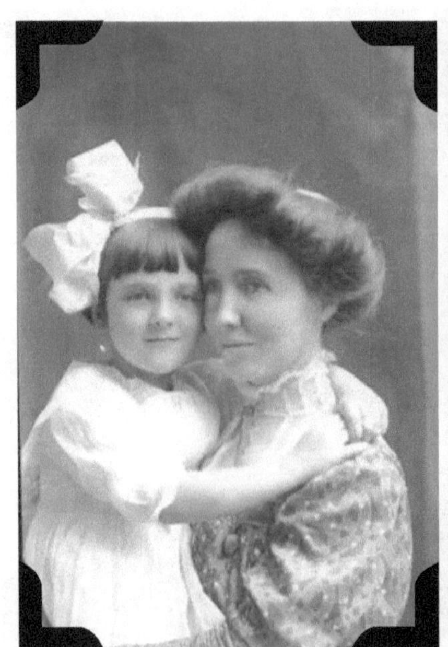

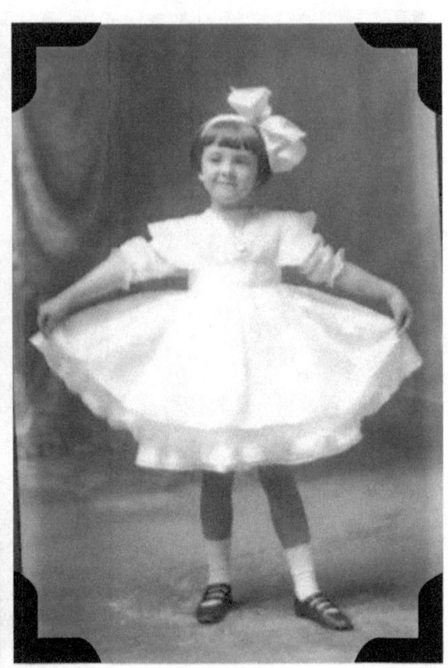

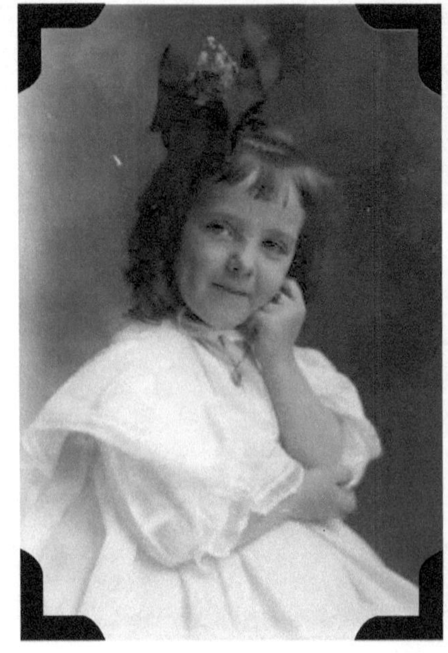

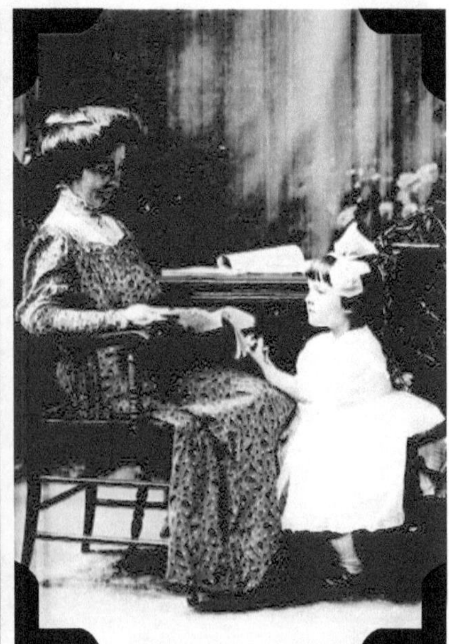

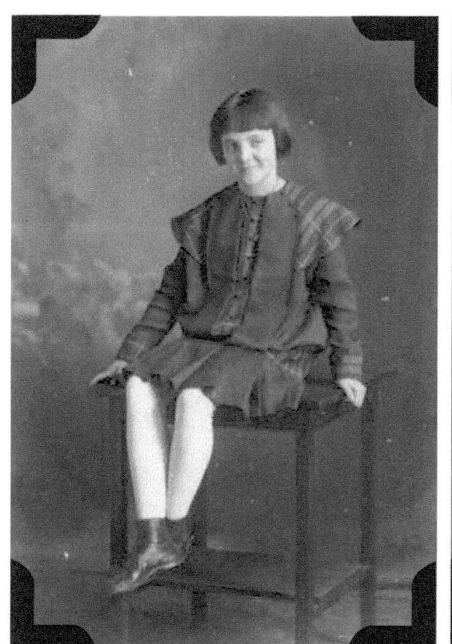

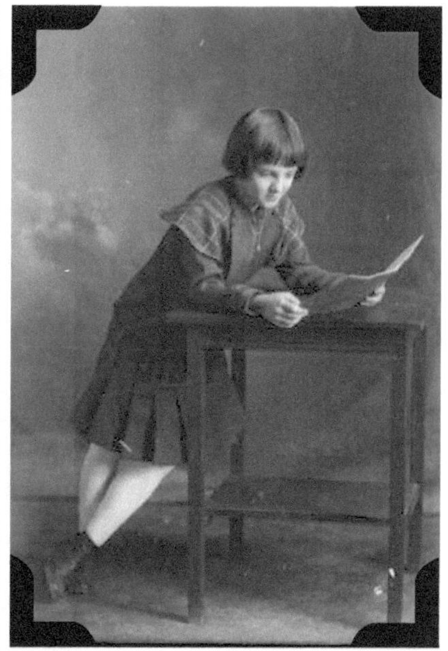

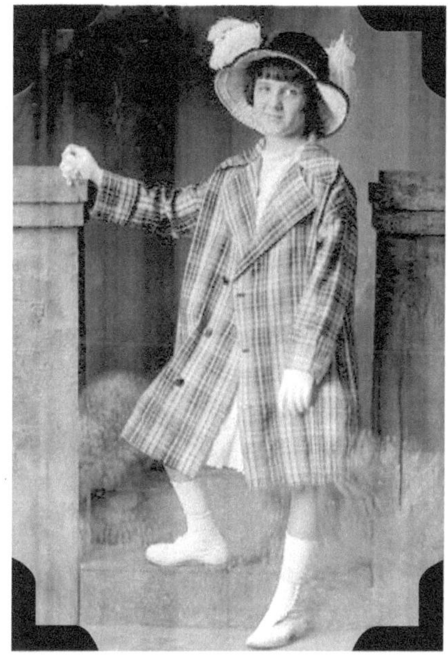

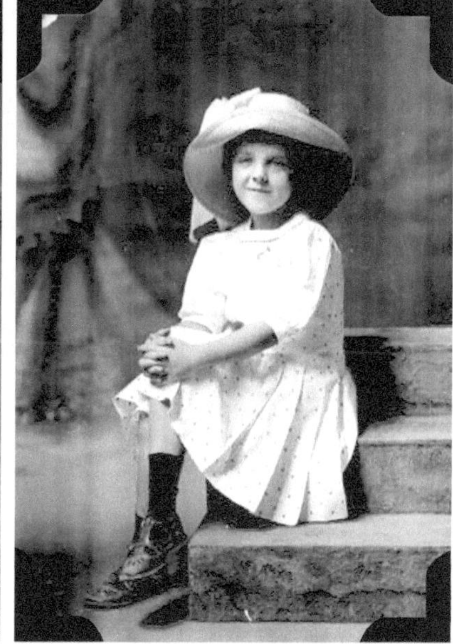

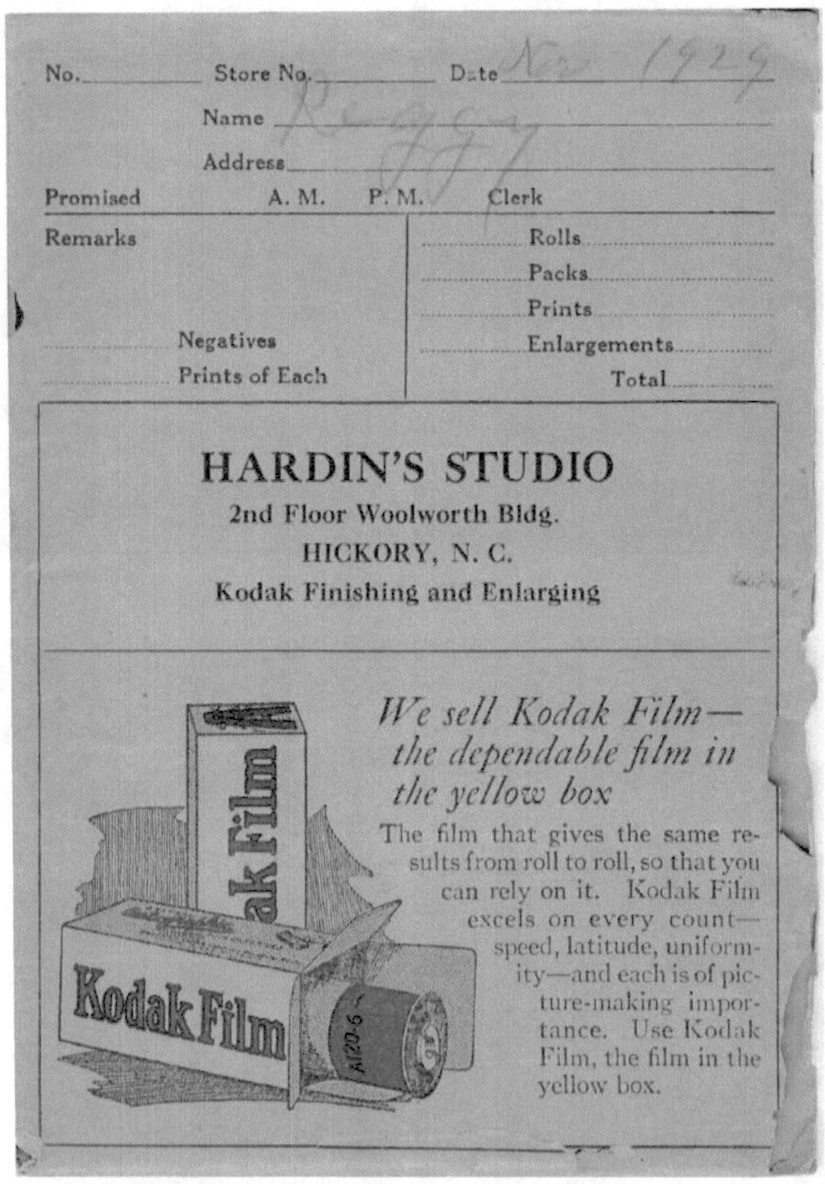

No.______ Store No.______ Date Nov 1929

Name Peggy

Address______

Promised A. M. P. M. Clerk

Remarks

......Negatives

......Prints of Each

......Rolls......

......Packs......

......Prints......

......Enlargements......

Total......

HARDIN'S STUDIO

2nd Floor Woolworth Bldg.

HICKORY, N. C.

Kodak Finishing and Enlarging

We sell Kodak Film—the dependable film in the yellow box

The film that gives the same results from roll to roll, so that you can rely on it. Kodak Film excels on every count—speed, latitude, uniformity—and each is of picture-making importance. Use Kodak Film, the film in the yellow box.

C.M. Hardin quickly became a respected member of the Hickory community. In addition to his business, C.M. joined the Hickory Military Opera Band, reported to be the first such organized musical group in town. They played regularly at the Union Square bandstand, as well as towns across the region. It was likely C.M.'s love of music that he hoped would translate to his daughter for her life's work. Instead, it was his other passion, his day job, that captivated her.

These are the tools of the photographic trade. In the early days of of commercial photography images were cast onto glass plates. The emulsion side of the plate was where the silver nitrate coalesced to form a negative image of the photograph. C.M. bought his from the M.A. Seed Dry Plate Company. The Hardin Studio used many dry plates, retaining them to make future prints. Boxes of them were so numerous that later, Kathryn used boxes of them as door stops. Images of many Hickory citizens were captured on those plates, in addition to C.M.'s own family.

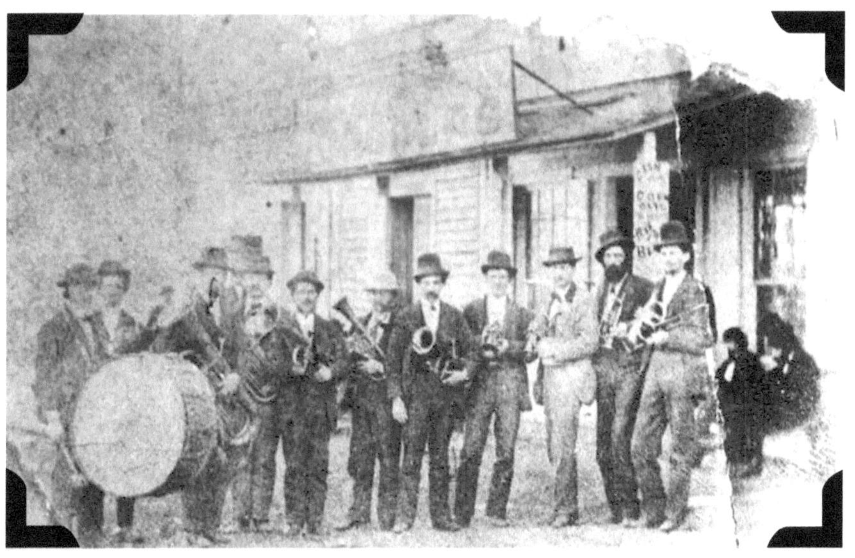

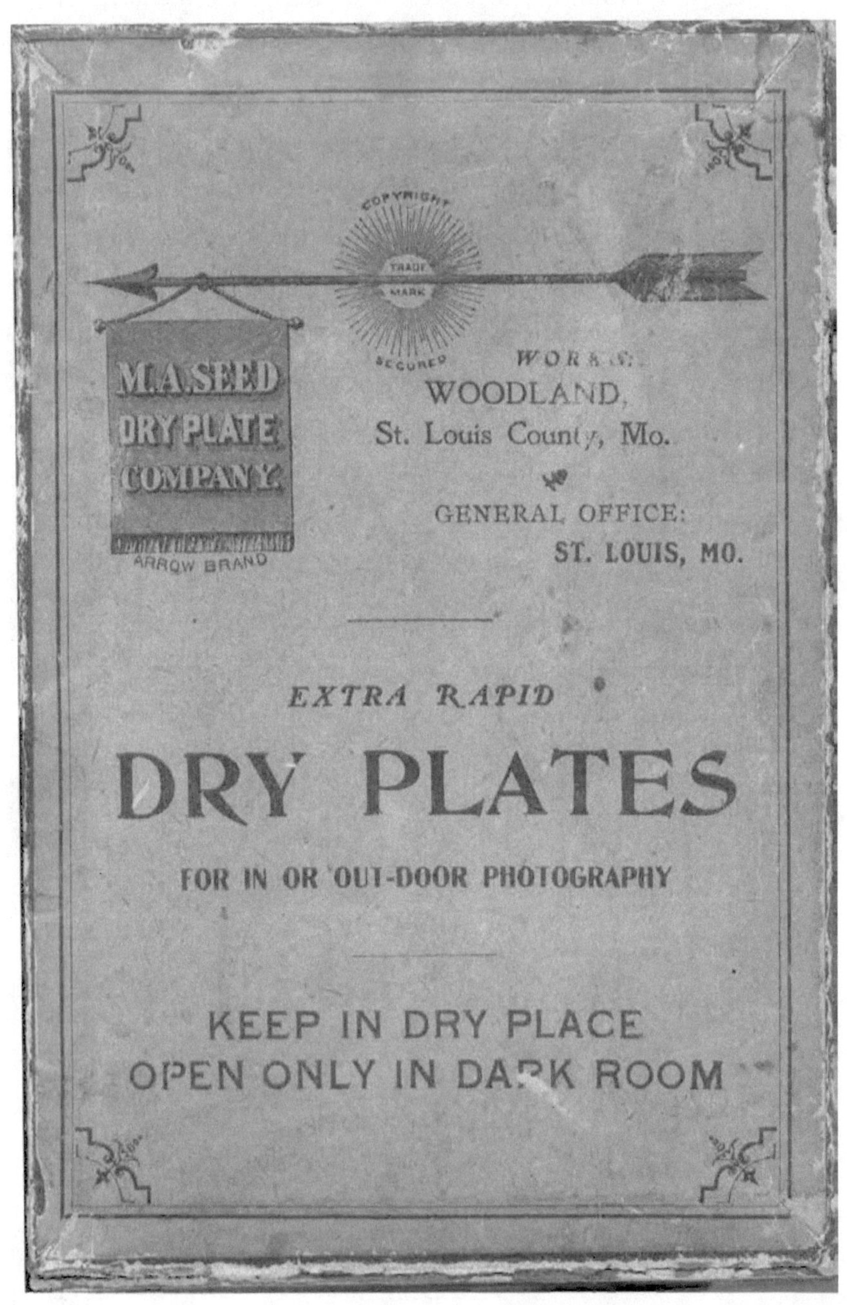
COPYRIGHT
TRADE MARK
SECURED
M.A. SEED
DRY PLATE
COMPANY.
ARROW BRAND
WOODLAND,
St. Louis County, Mo.
GENERAL OFFICE:
ST. LOUIS, MO.
EXTRA RAPID
DRY PLATES
FOR IN OR OUT-DOOR PHOTOGRAPHY
KEEP IN DRY PLACE
OPEN ONLY IN DARK ROOM

Later, when celluloid film became the standard, the Hardin Studio converted to the thinner negatives, which were more easily stored for future use. In the early 20th century, photography was being revolutionized by the Eastman Kodak Company. George Eastman had made every photographers life easier, introducing smaller cameras to the market. When the local paper created a baby photo contest, C.M. was there to snap the shot. In 1918, Kodak sponsored a promotion to get cameras in the hands of America's youth by giving away 48 in Hickory. The Hardin studio "offered to develop each of these first films free for the children."

As the photography business continued to attract more paying customers, the Hardins moved up the societal ladder. They first bought the home of Hickory pioneer J.W. Elliott in the Kenwood neighborhood before purchasing the spacious house of K.C. Menzies, preeminent banker in town. This home, dubbed Greencourt, stood at the intersection of Center Street and First Avenue. After Kathryn married and had her own daughter, she became the model of choice for C.M., who steps from behind the camera to be photographed with his granddaughter Peggy on the front stoop of the home.

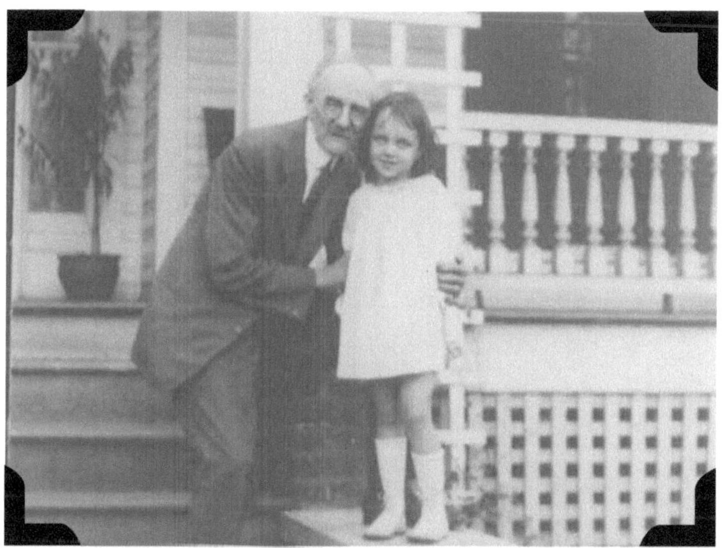

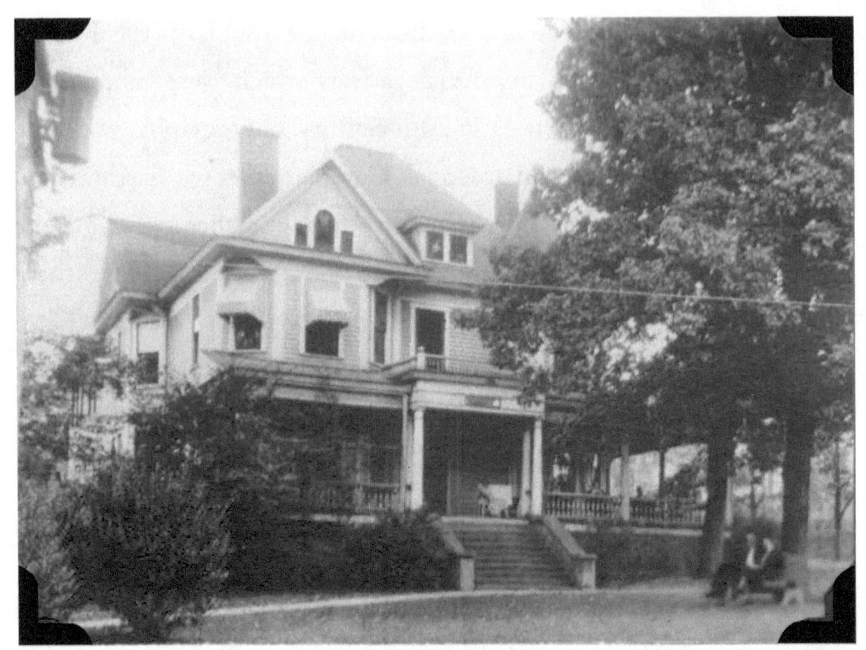

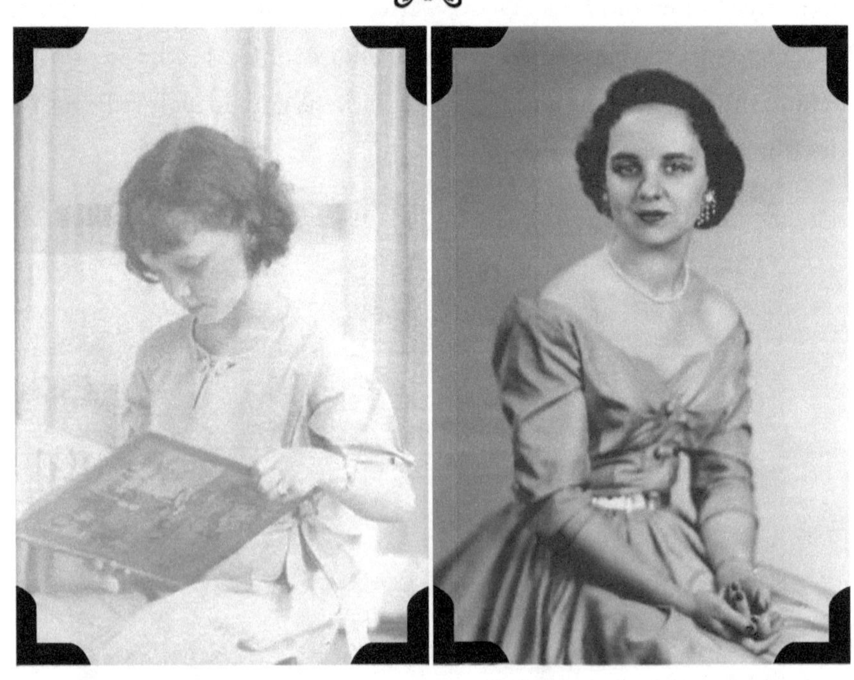

As with most images of the era, C.M. shot in black and white. Leona handled the administration of the business, and when Kathryn showed an interest in adding color to some images by hand painting them, she worked after school to learn how. Later, she recalled the process of tinting pictures as her "favorite part of the work." C.M. wanted his daughter to become a musician. While Kathryn sang "Oh Promise Me" at the Hickory Academy of Music at age 9, she left behind a music career to join with her parents at Hardin Studio. A graduate of Meredith College in Raleigh, C.M. recognized his daughter's interest in the visual arts was stronger than music, so he found noted professionals to train his her in the burgeon art of photography.

The three favorite subjects of C.M. Hardin, likely taken in 1943. Seated is mother, Leona. Daughter Kathryn sits on the arm of the chair while Peggy stands behind, comprising three generations of Hardins. Like her mother, Peggy grew up in front of a camera, her toddler days photographed by her grandfather, later her mother. Below is a tinted image of Kathryn and Peggy as she came of age.

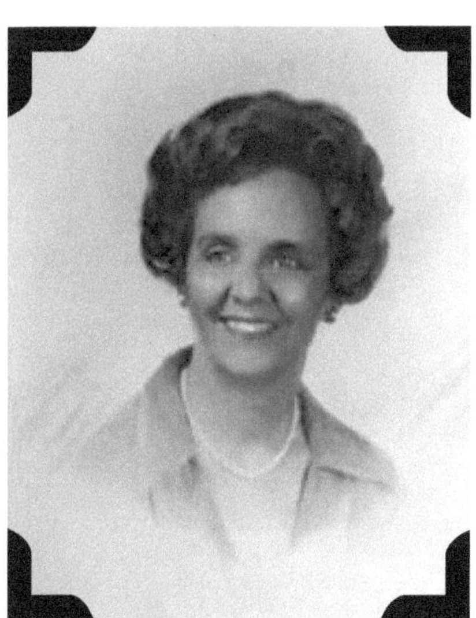

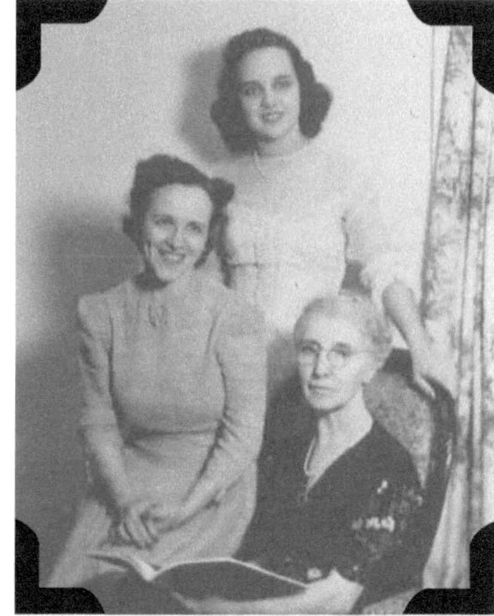

CHAPTER 2

THE FIRE

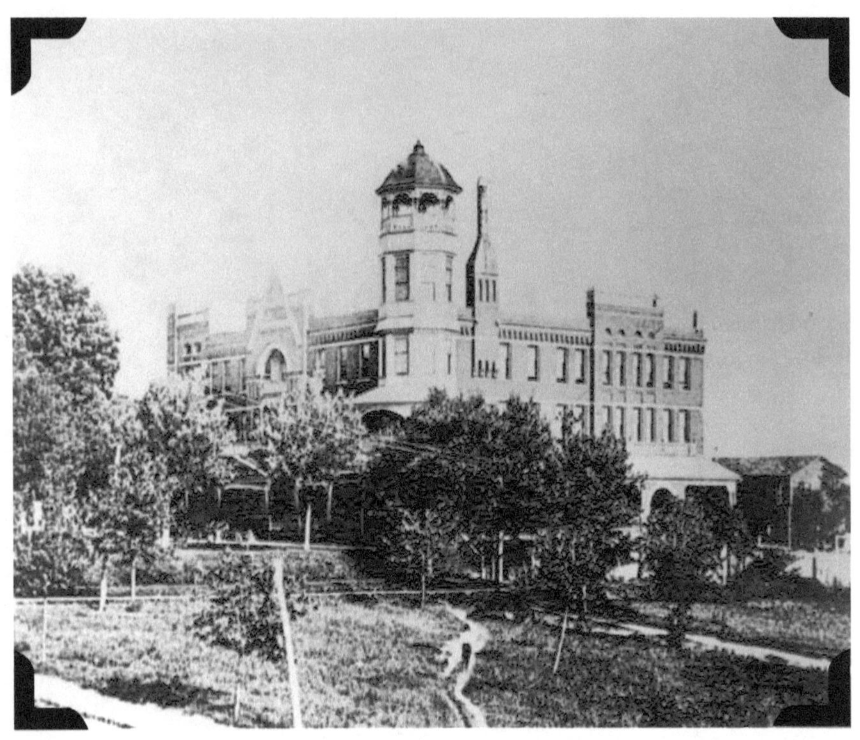

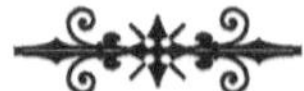

With the completion of the Hickory Inn in 1888, the town for which the hotel was named became an important destination. From a stopover along the stagecoach line, Hickory Tavern found its place on the map with the arrival of the railroad in 1860, the site of a Confederate storage facility during the Civil War, and incorporation into a town five years after the conclusion of the conflict.

When constructed, the Hickory Inn offered all the amenities available to a 19th century traveler. Fine dining, luxurious accommodations (by Victorian standards), but perhaps most importantly, a grand view of the Blue Ridge Mountains. Since no transportation source of the time could easily carry tourists to the high country, vacationers had to be content with the vistas to be seen to the north and west of town. Builders of the Hickory Inn understood the attraction. Atop the four story structure guests enjoyed a birds eye view of the mountains in a specially constructed cupola. Sightseers could also watch fellow guests and townsfolk while they strolled the streets below, spending weeks each summer in a climate Hickory citizens believed was perfect for enjoyment, elevated just enoughto protect from the miasmic maladies of the lowlands, but short of mountain borne diseases that brought on rheumatism and rickets.

With its gaze firmly fixed on the future, Hickory citizens believed they had tapped into a key attraction of the region. The wealth brought by this burgeoning tourist industry established western North Carolina as the perfect locale for regenerative rest and relaxation. The Hickory Inn soon became known as the finest hotel between Asheville and Salisbury, a place to compete with the resort of Catawba Springs (another Catawba County destination) just eight miles to the northeast of Hickory.

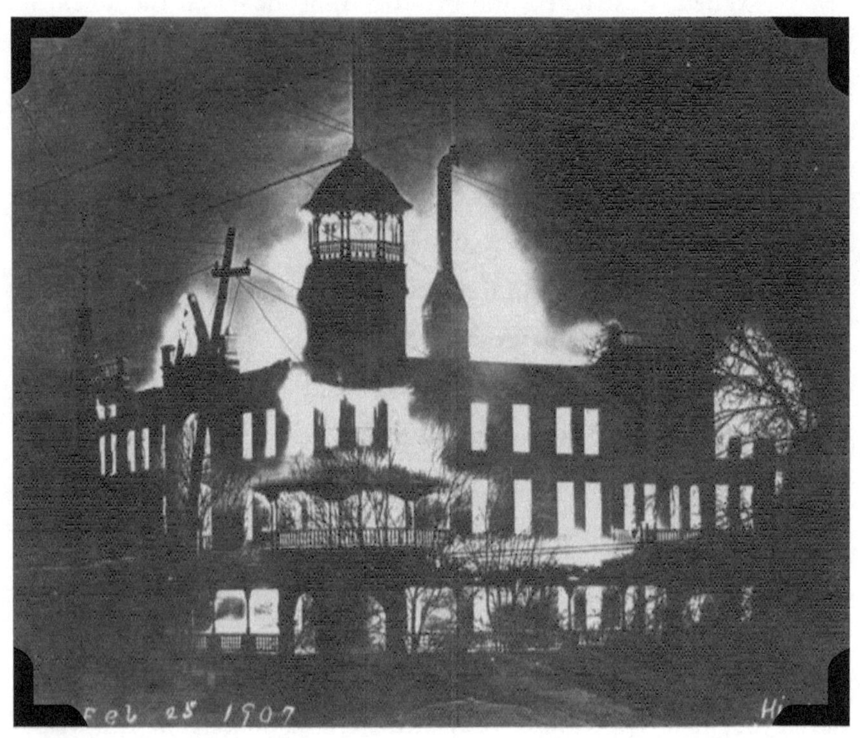
Feb 25 1907

In the predawn hours of February 28, 1907, fire engulfed the Hickory Inn. Some accounts reported "the explosion of a lamp" in the "servant's quarters" as the cause, while others said the blaze originated in the dining room, or perhaps a cloakroom. Though constructed of brick, everything else was wood and fabric and went up quickly in the flames.

As soon as alerted, a hotel employee went door to door, beseeching guests to get out quickly. Before it could be evacuated, the fire consumed the interior of the building. Exits were blocked, forcing some patrons to leap from the windows of their rooms to get out. Four men sustained broken bones from jumping. Arriving firemen heroically used ladders to bring others to safety. Survivors reported "many narrow escapes" from the burning building. No one died in the fire, but property damage was extensive.

As the sun rose on that winter morning, survivors huddled, often without shoes or warm clothing to watch the fire finish its consumption of their luggage and all its contents."Practically all the contents of hotel was burned," reported one newspaper. Damage was estimated at $50,000, equivalent to over $1.75 million almost 120 years later. Insurance on the building totaled less than a third of its actual value. The calamity was a significant blow to Hickory's growth and prestige.

It was reported that a passerby first noticed the fire and sounded the alarm. Possibly, that citizen was C.M. Hardin. If not, he was among the first to witness the blaze. Rushing to his Union Square photography studio, he grabbed his camera and snapped the most newsworthy image of his entire career, the fire at its devastating apex. Against the early morning sky, the brick outline of the Hickory Inn is dark with the raging flames providing the only light.

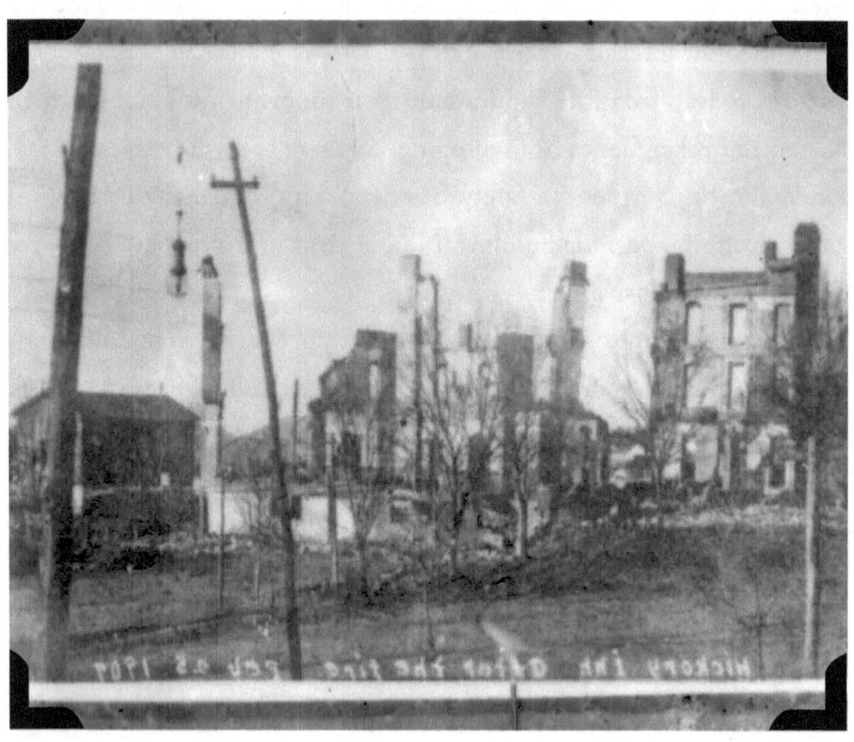

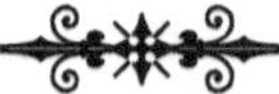

C.M. Hardin knew he had captured an incredible moment in the life of the town. At some point after the embers had cooled and the smoke cleared, he returned again to record a more detailed look at the ruins. Daylight revealed that only the brick portions of the hotel remained. With this shot, Hardin completed a trilogy of images, detailing the life and death of Hickory's greatest landmark of its time.

Many of the guests that night were traveling salesmen, or drummers as they were euphemistically known since they were in Hickory to 'drum up' business. In the aftermath, one man, a Mr. Goldsmith from Cincinnati, called for regulation from state officials to prevent another such mishap. He pointed out how the Hickory Inn had "no fire escapes, no electric bells and no one on night duty to look after the safety of sleeping and helpless guests." The last assertion was an overstatement since it was J.E. Montague, proprietor of the hotel who ran upstairs to awaken sleeping guests. Montague found himself trapped when the flames cut off his exit, requiring him to jump from a second story window. He landed on "hard cement pavement...seriously injuring his spine."

In the days after the fire, a number of stories emerged about the confusion of the early morning catastrophe. William McCaw was spending his last night of bachelorhood at the Hickory Inn, planning to be married the next day to Genevieve Anderson. Awakened by the clamor of everyone escaping, he fled too, only to realize that he left the marriage license in his room. He quickly weighed his options. It was either take another trip to the county seat of Newton to get a second license or ging back into the burning building to retrieve the first one. He chose the latter. Venturing back inside, the confusion of the moment temporarily landed him in the wrong room, costing him valuable seconds he might need on his second exit. McCaw remained determined, though. He not only luckily gained his bearings and found the right room, in addition to locating the license, he also took a moment to find his pants and the "wad" (presumably money) pocketed in them before finding his way out, again.

The last man out of the building was E.O. Hinson of Baltimore. His room on the third floor had been cut off by the fire. With "coolness and presence of mind," he threw his "grip" (suitcase) out of the window first. Then, "he dressed himself, and seeing that the ice-coating on the ledge would prevent his escape," he tied a coverlet and blanket together "and with the other end around his waist, swung out and caught the ladder."

The work of C.M. Hardin has insured that this historical event, one pivotal to the development of Hickory, would not be forgotten. He was not a news photographer by any stretch of the imagination. In fact, his primary focus revolved around local faces. That was his business model. However, when such a huge opportunity presents itself, he grasped the value of immortalizing the event, forevermore.

CHAPTER 3

AROUND TOWN

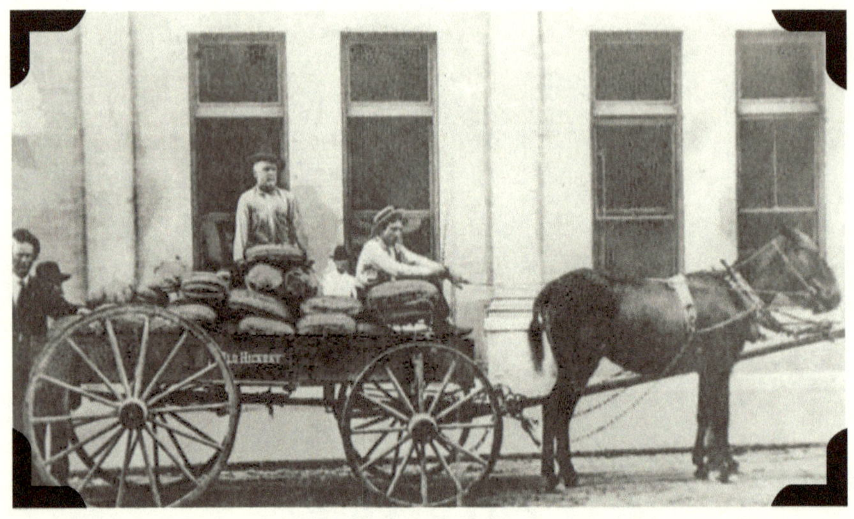

During the years that C.M. Hardin took pictures, Hickory emerged as a bustling regional center of commerce. Union Square, still today the center of activity in the city, was the preferred desti- nation of produce growers, ready to sell their crops. So many farmers came down from outlying farms like these men, that the gathering spot was once known popularly as Park Place. Not dissimilar from today's farmers market, folks came to buy and sell. In this image, a load of watermelons has arrived on a Piedmont Wagon, which was manufactured in Hickory.

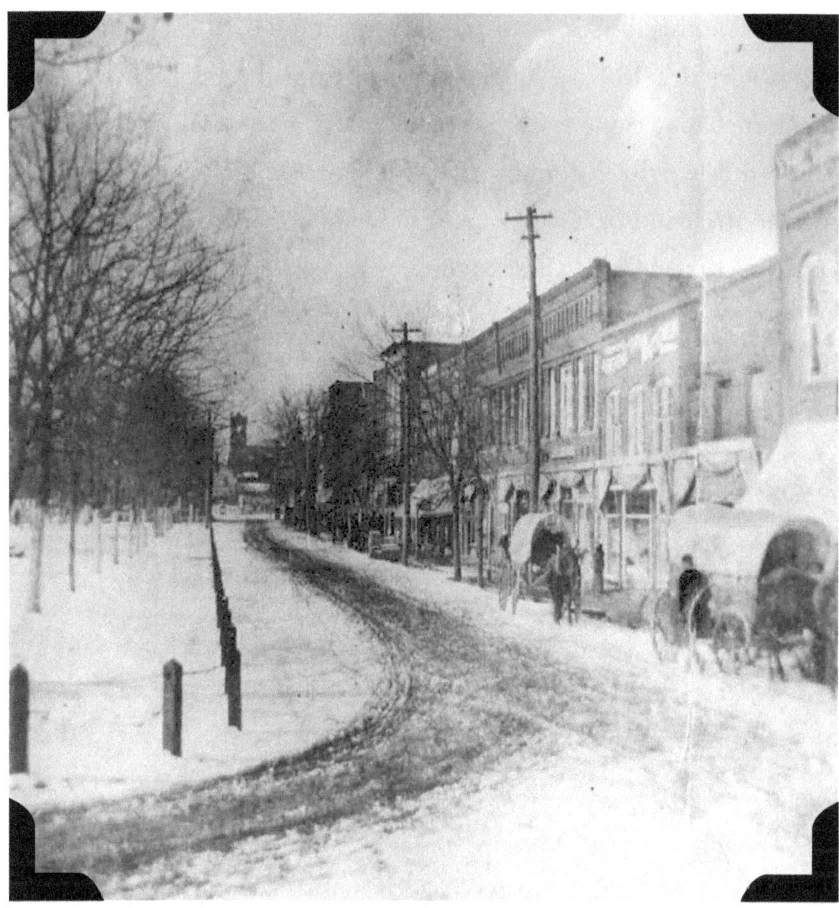

In the era before automobiles, this is the way Union Square looked during the winter. Looking east to west, many of the brick structures featured here still stand. At the far end of the street is the old First Baptist Church. While the church has since retained the entire block for its sanctuary, offices and Sunday School rooms, the bell tower (seen here) was torn down, reorienting the church toward what is now Second Avenue Northwest The trees on the left mark the commons area that stood between the storefronts and the railroad tracks. Many changes have taken place over the years in downtown, but the open space has remained a hallmark.

Another image from the early years of C.M. Hardin's career in Hickory. It's 1902, a different season from the previous but once again the Union Square serves as a backdrop. These two ladies (Maude Shuford driving) are donning their Sunday best for a trip to town. A regular attraction in down- town Hickory were band concerts and ice cream socials which established the area as a place to see and be seen.

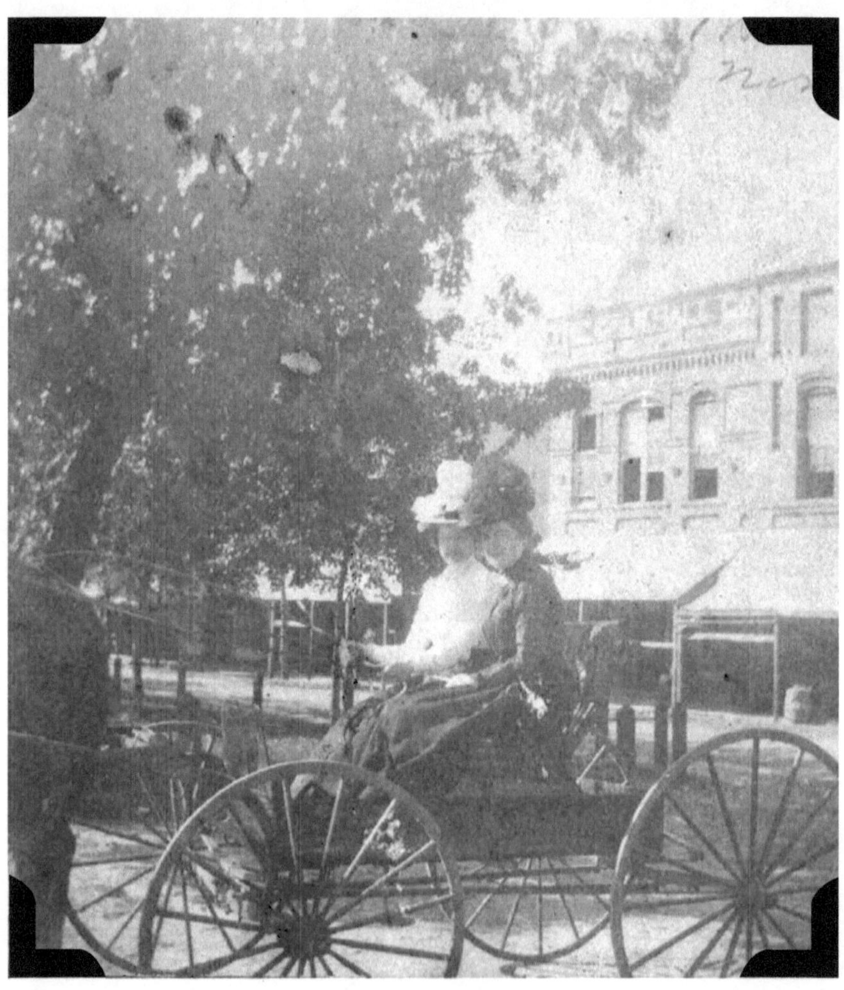

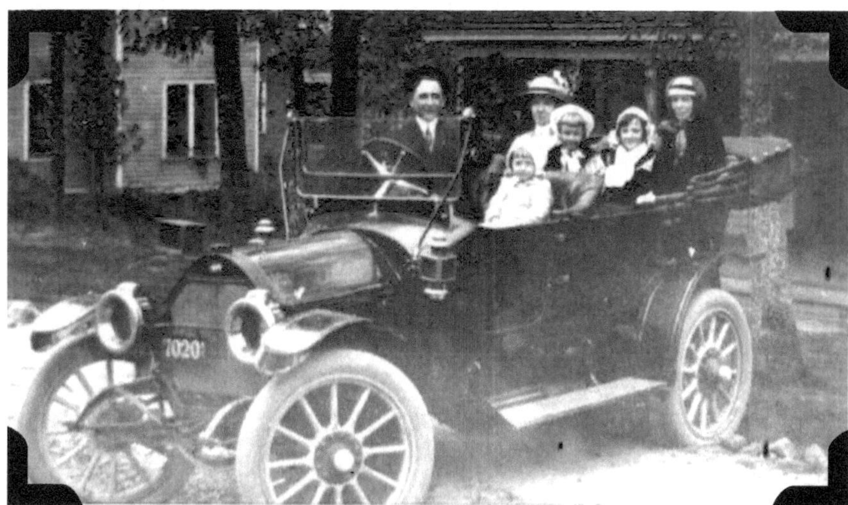

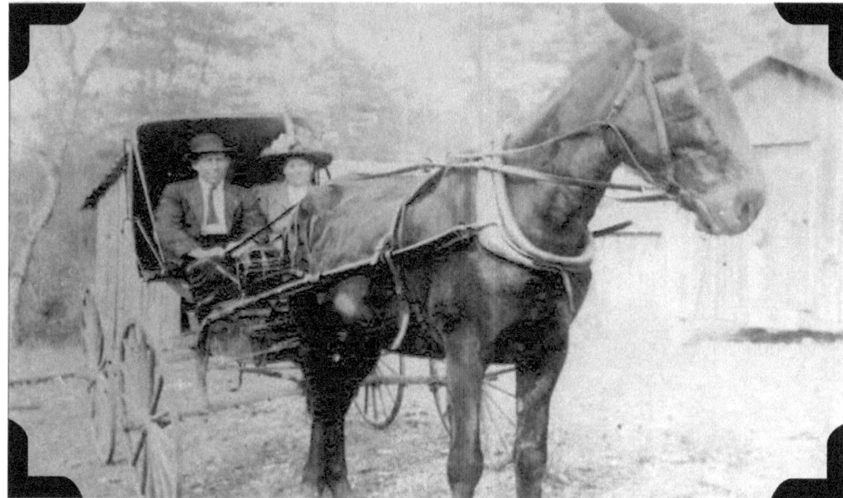

Two ways to get around in Hickory. Both photographed by C.M. Hardin, the top image of Mr. and Mrs. Joseph Mull shows the couple dressed for a visit. The same can be said of the I.A. Wood family, only they are traveling from home in what was reported to be one of Hickory's first auto-mobiles. Horse or horsepower, the times were a'changing.

Two of Hickory's early churches. Even before Hickory incorporated in 1870, places of worship were well established. Baptist, Methodist and German Reformed (Church of Christ) denominations were joined by Lutheran, Pres-byterian, Episcopalian and other congregations. Over the years, all have built larger sanctuaries to replace these earlier structures.

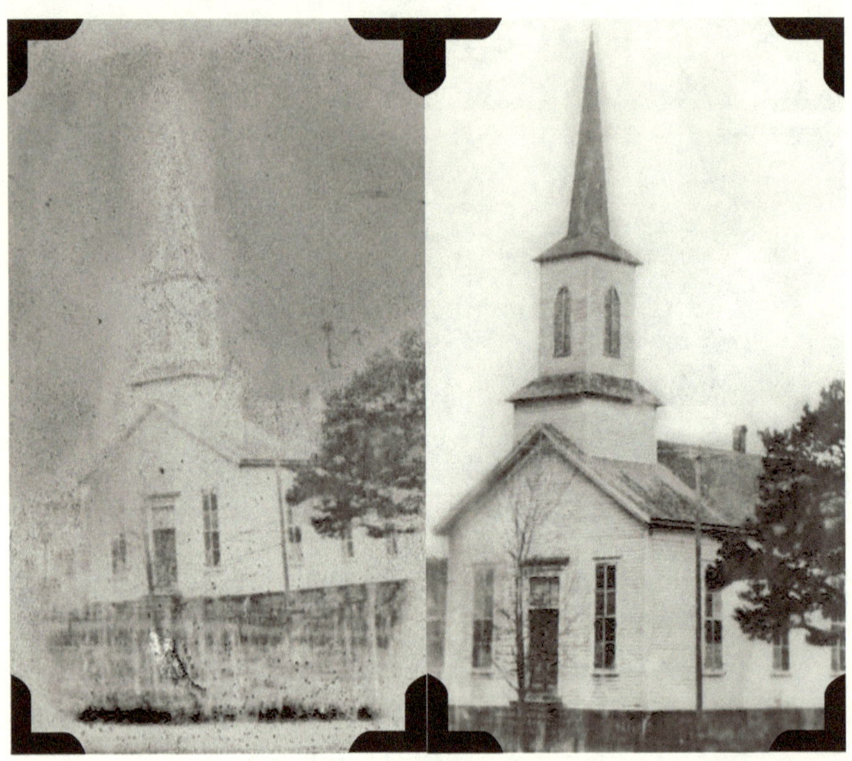

Claremont Female College below occupied the hill where the Salt Block now stands in northeast Hickory. It was started by Corinth Re- formed Church and patterned after Wellesley College in Massachusetts, as an educational outlet for women. The school operated from 1880- 1916. This building was completed in 1883, with an expansion added in 1888. Operation of the school ran moderately well with classes offered in science, literature, music, business and other disciplines, leading to both undergraduate and graduate degrees.

The school did however, experience a number of changes in leadership, which led to instability. Additionally, feared competition from another institution of higher learning, Catawba College in Newton, caused the church governing body to withdraw its support for Claremont. By 1916, Catawba was accepting female day students and with spring graduation that year, Hickory's only women's college shut down. The Reformed Church gave the site to the city for construction of a high school that opened in 1925, maintaining the property's status as a place for learning. The students below gathered for a Hardin photograph in the latter days of Claremont's existence.

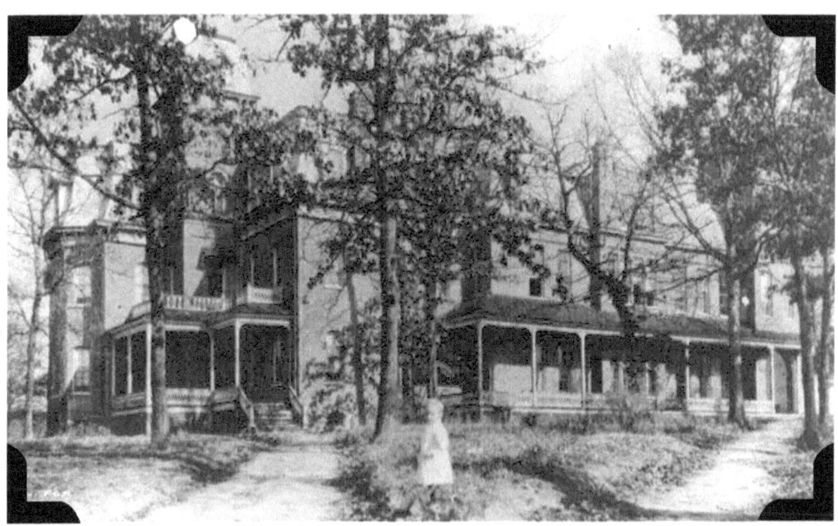

Successor to Claremont Women's College. The high school operated from 1925-1972. Citizens were justly proud of the new edifice which cost over $100,000 to build. Called "one of the finest remaining examples of the classical revival period of the early 20th century," the school opened with 14 instructors and 400 students. These photos were taken by Kathryn Hardin Whitener during the latter days of the school.

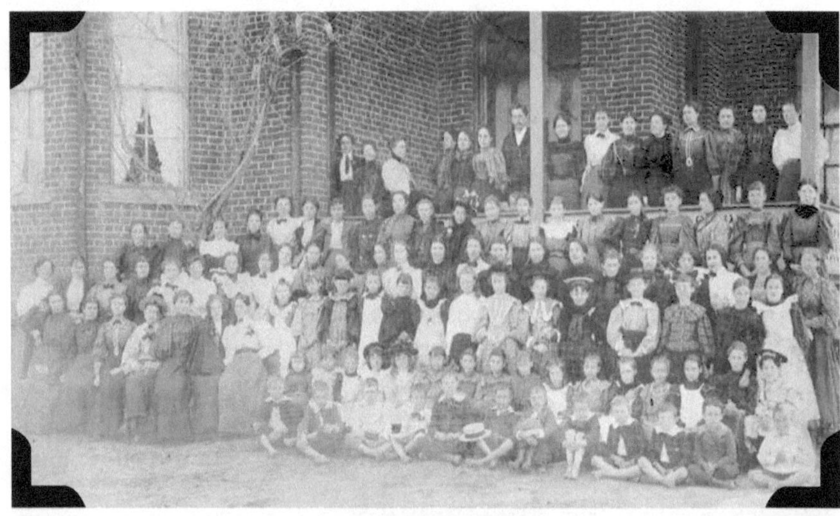

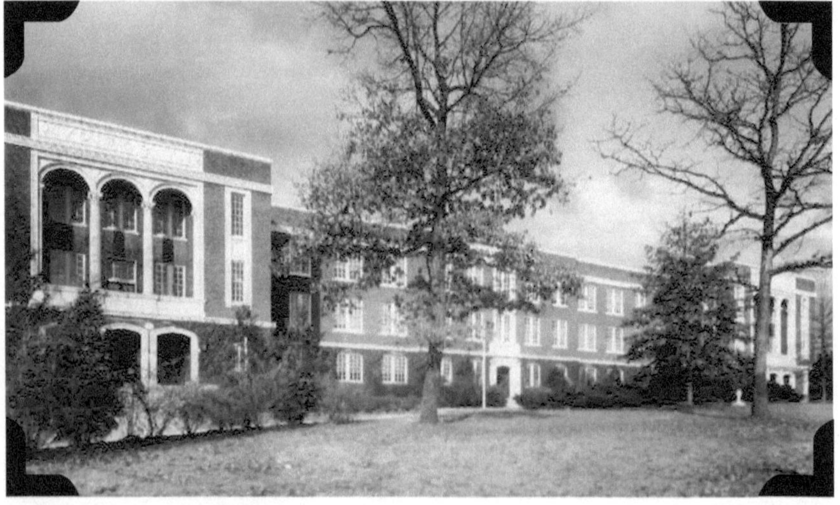

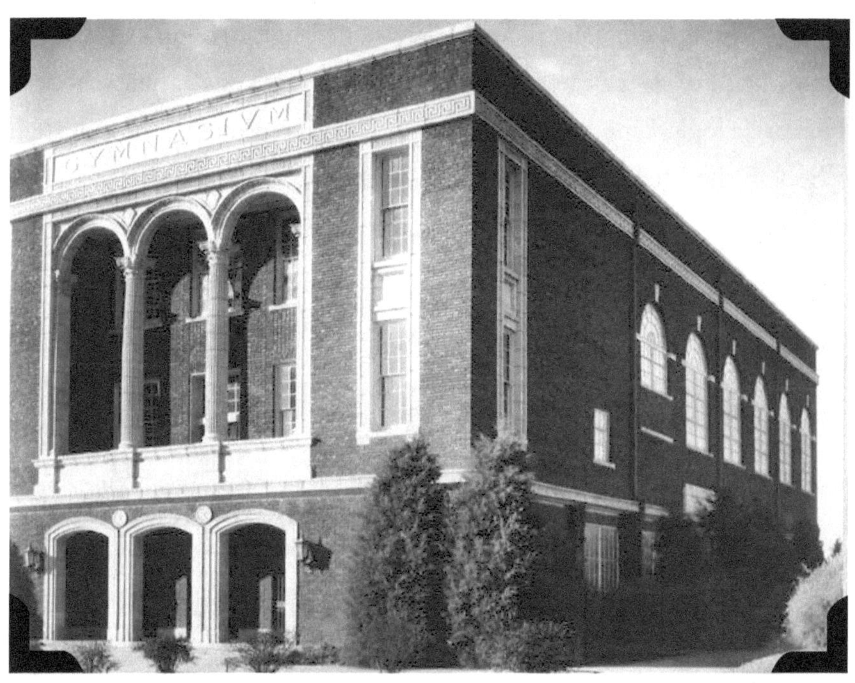
GYMNASIVM

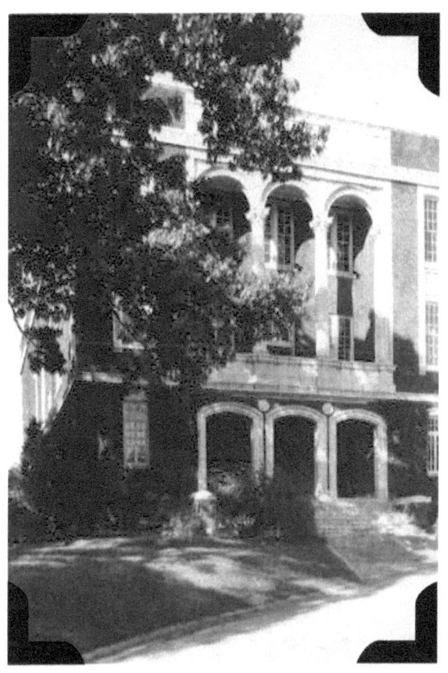

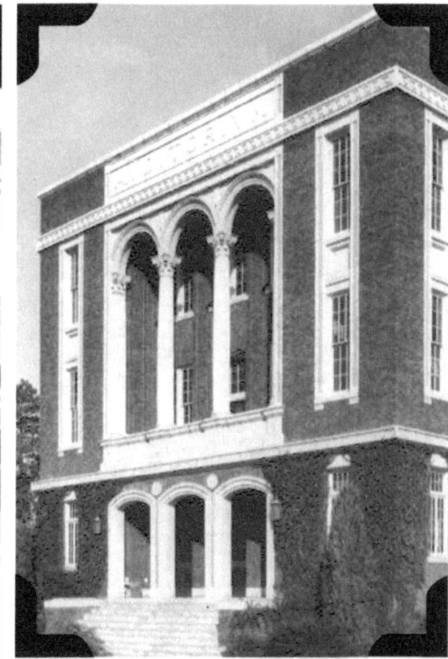

Though officially named Claremont High School, as the letter on the front of the sweater indicates, students referred to their school as Hickory, a logical choice since the school was (and remains) the only high school in the Hickory City System. These undated pics show members of the Mono-gram Club posing in front of the Hardin camera.

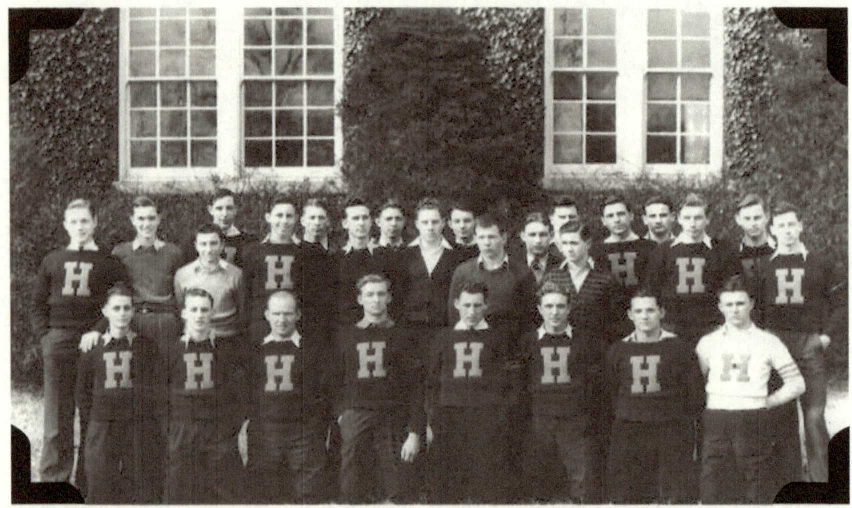

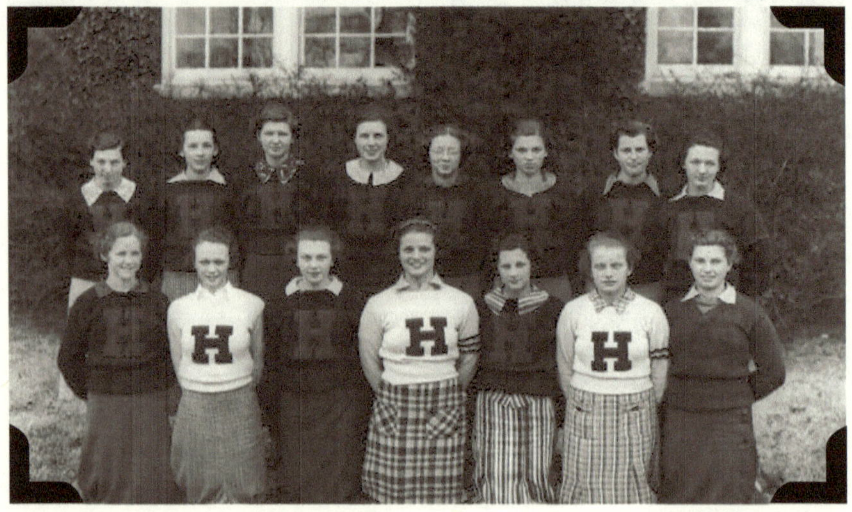

Before students entered Claremont High School they were a part of the Hickory Graded School System. These undated class photos show principal, teacher and pupils gathered on the front steps in their finest, ready for picture day.

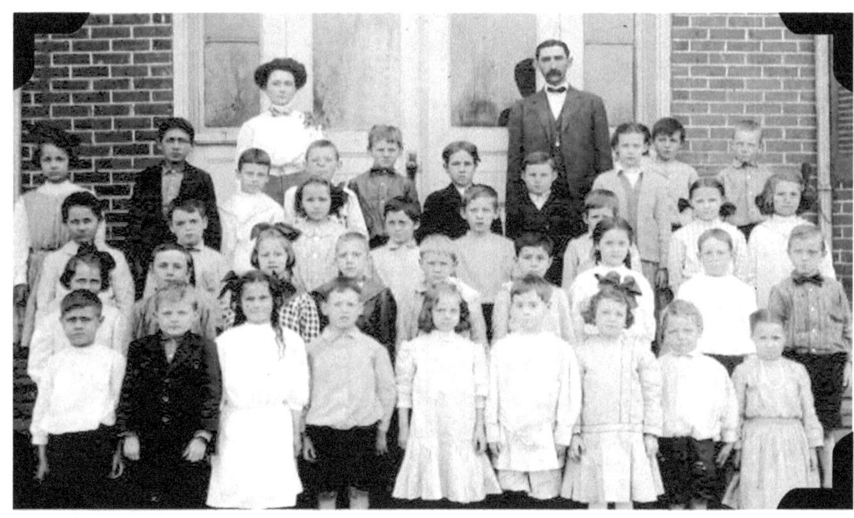

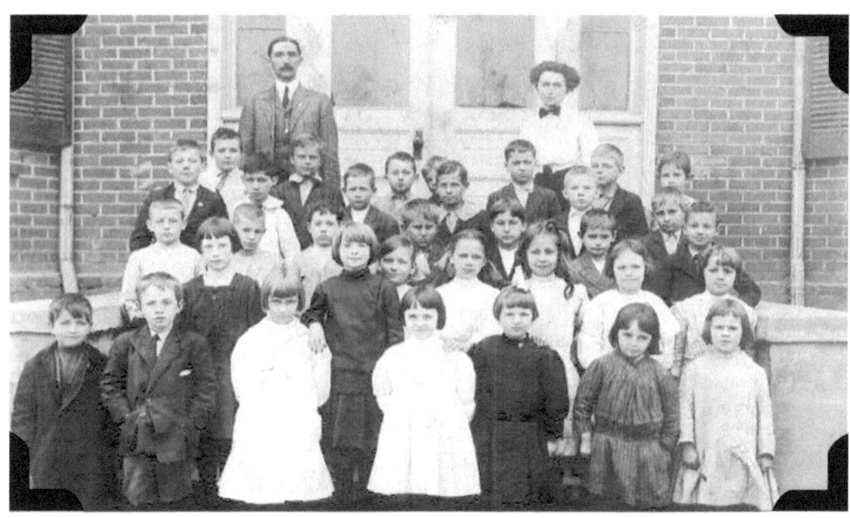

Both ends of the world of education. Above, graduates of an earlier era pose for their last picture before applying their studies in various ways. It would be interesting to conjecture that perhaps one of those individuals might also be featured in the image below, among the faculty of Lenoir-Rhyne college during a later era.

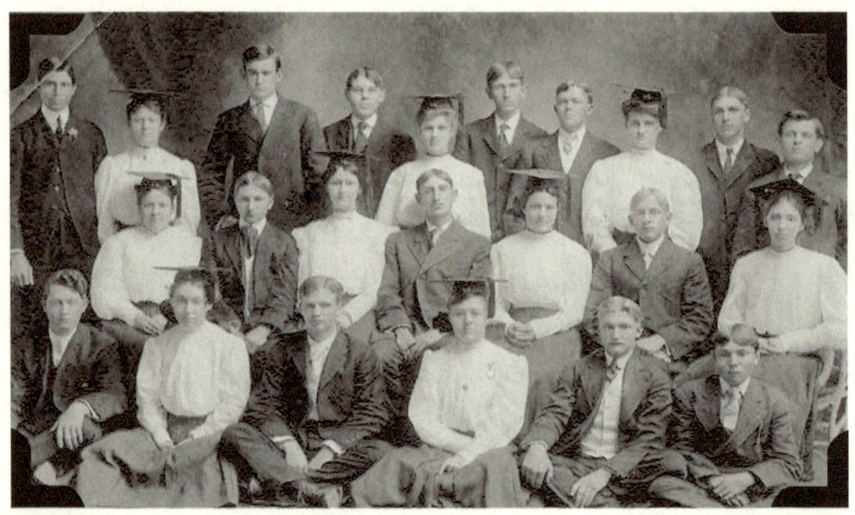

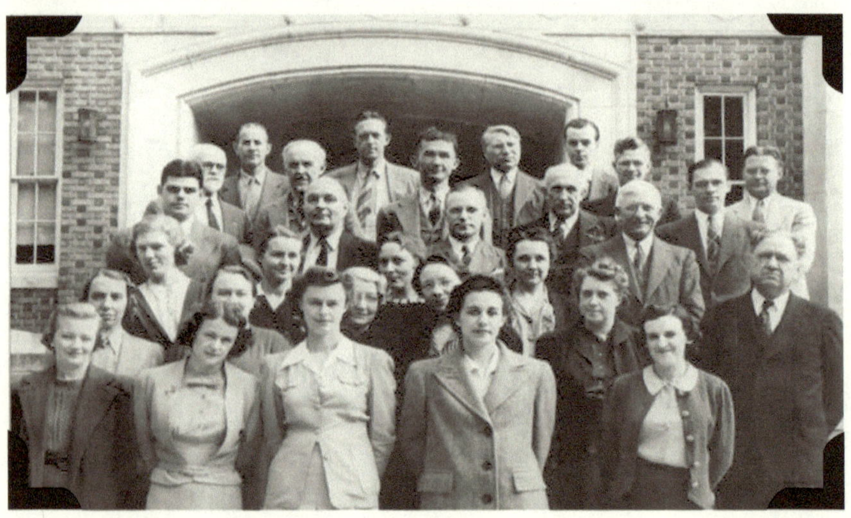

Extracurricular life on the campus of Lenoir - Rhyne College.

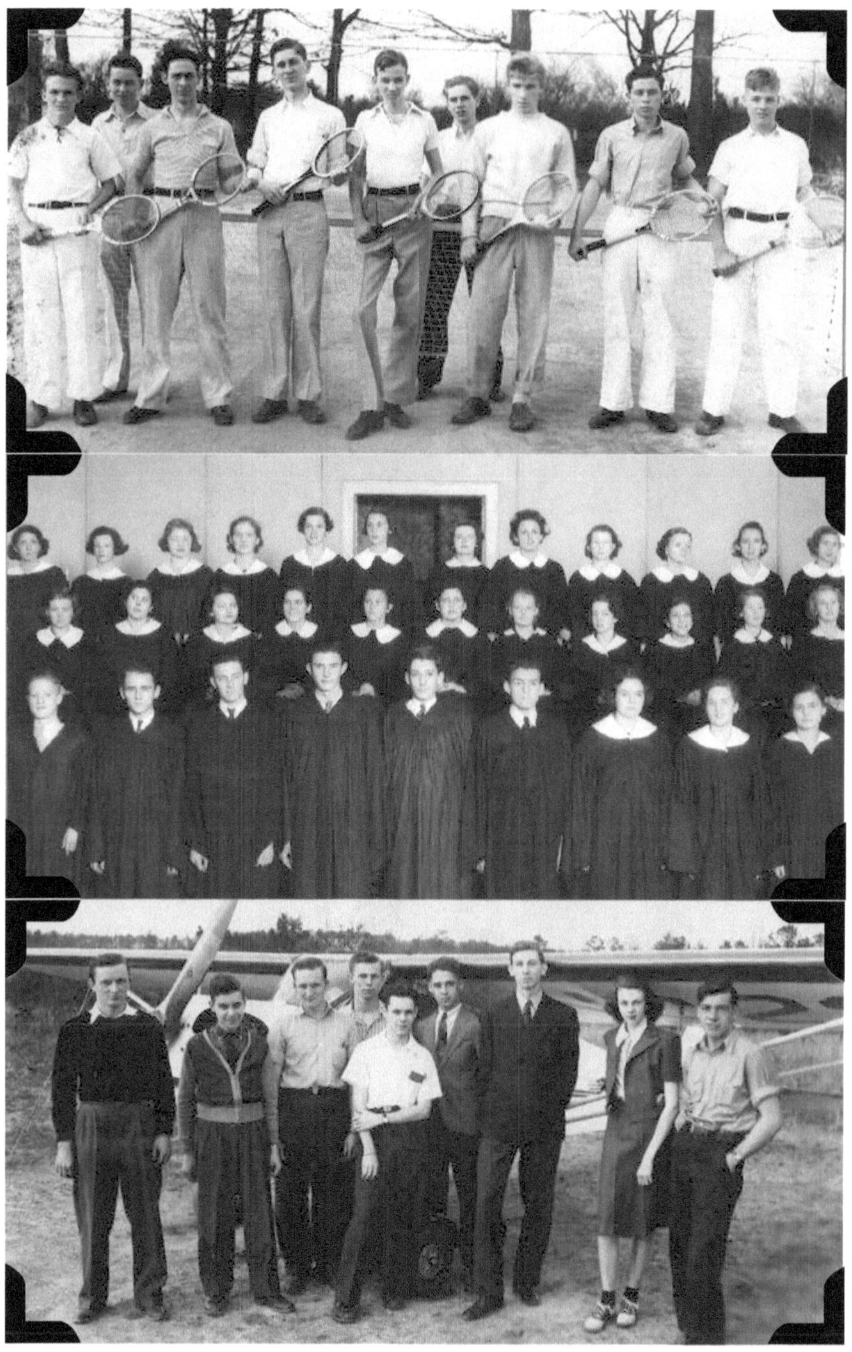

Developing skills. How many of the children posing for this picture in front of the Hickory Graded School would one day hone their musical skills to one day performing for the Hickory High Band?

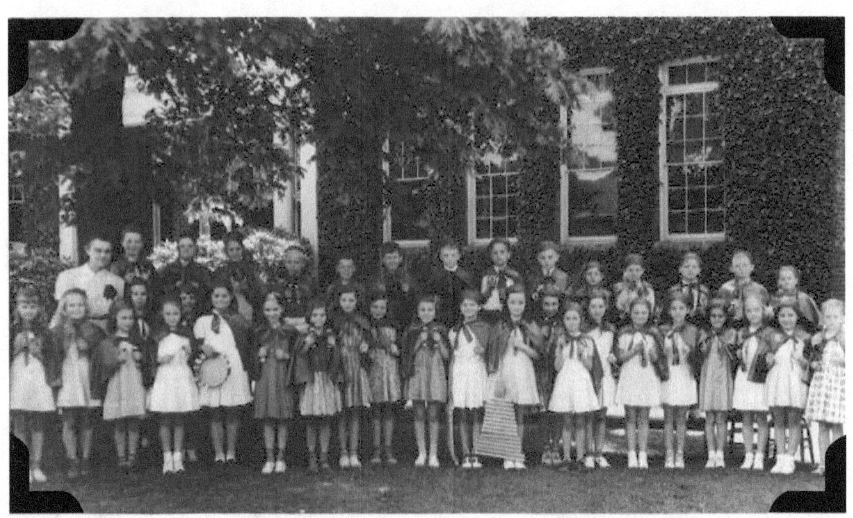

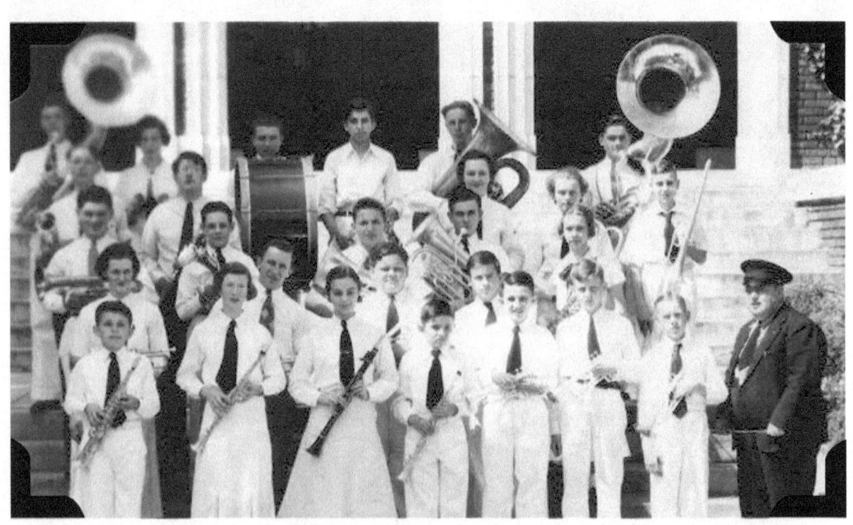

Employees of Shuford Mills, approximately 1910. Workers of all ages gathered at the back of the mill for a photo. Started in 1880 by A. A. Shuford, his first cotton refining plant in Granite Falls spawned a number of related enterprises beyond yarn and cordage.

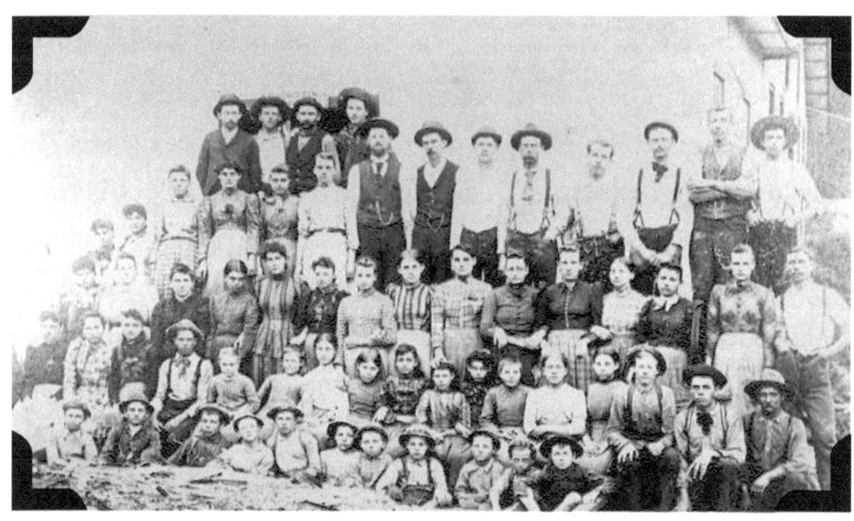

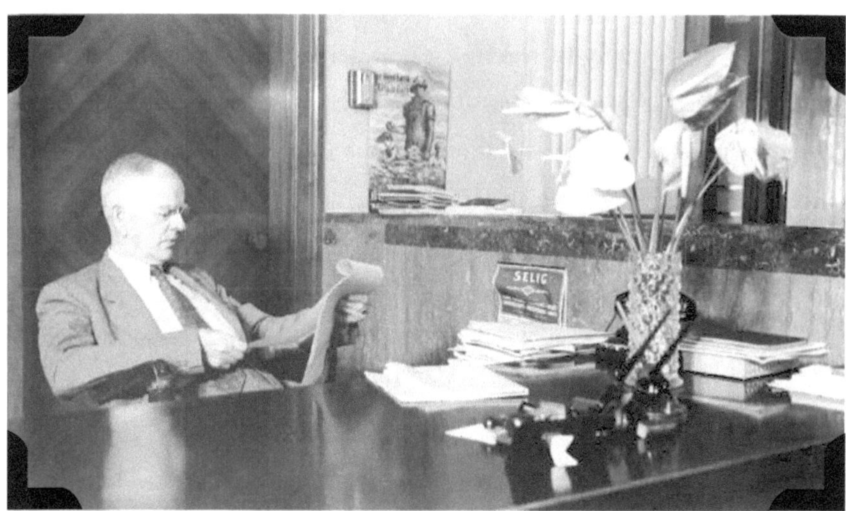

If you were to walk into the First National Bank of Catawba County in 1944, this is the scene you might see. Seated and reading a document is Mr. K. C. Menzies, the head of the bank. According to his granddaughter Evelyn Beam, you could set your watch by his movements. Every working day, Mr. Menzies walked home from the bank at lunch at precisely the same time and back again. He lived across from the old Hickory High.

Menzies had been a part of Hickory banking since the very first years of the city's existence. D. W. Shuler started the Bank of Hickory in 1886 and hired a young K.C. to be the teller. When the bank turned insolvent in the summer of 1890 and Shuler died as a result (some say he faked his death), the First National Bank of Hickory (later Catawba County) replaced the failed bank with Menzies. He was not implicated in the Shuler bank, and rose to the position of president of the bank.

K. C. Menzies was regarded as a careful, but fair man who guided Hickory to financial stability. Just another working day at the Esprit d'Amour Beauty Shop.

As with many of the images, understanding why these photos were taken remains a mystery. It's likely that the business wanted this scene documented either to show off the equipment or the attentive service received by beauticians at the "Spirit of Love" salon.

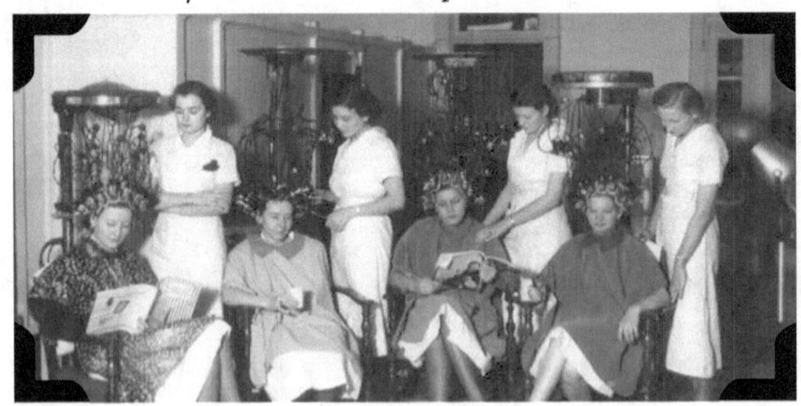

Bygone Hickory businesses. A rare aerial shot, below revealing the expanse of the Howard-Hickory Nursery. It started as a small operation by O.J. Howard, who had moved to the outskirts of West Hickory in 1920. His nursery grew to encompass three farms (150 acres) as sales increased. Over one-half million plants were estimated to be growing in either the greenhouses or on the lot within six years of the opening of the company. In the early 1960s, the large expanse of land was sold and a factory was built on the land. Below, the men of Lipe Motor Lines assemble for a group photo.

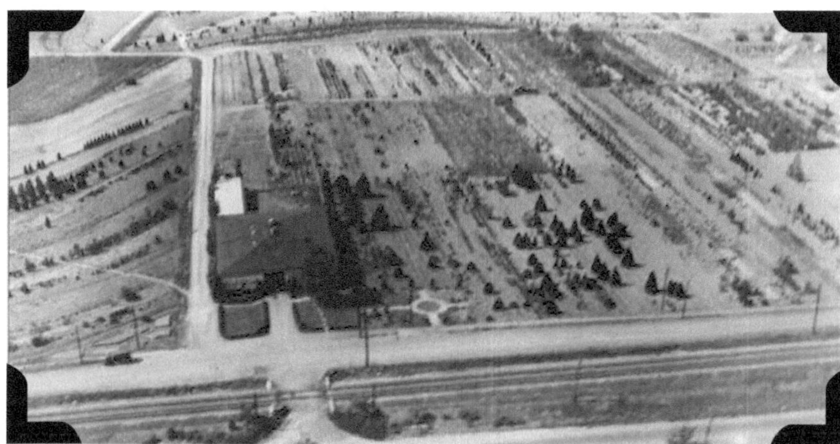

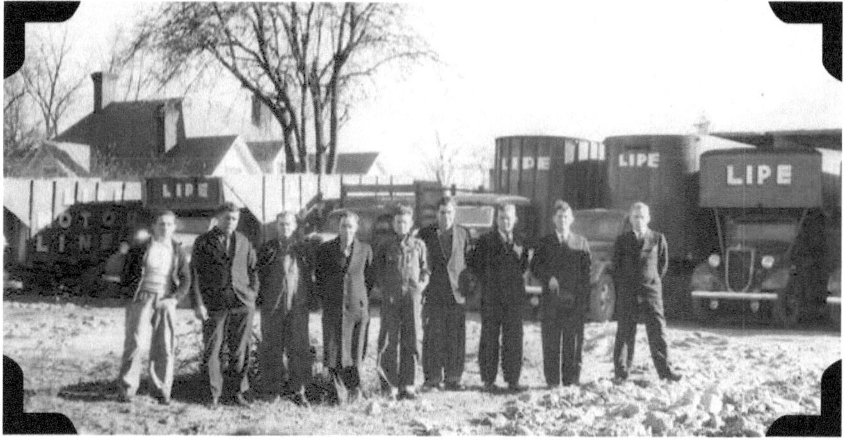

M.P. Lipe moved to Hildebran about the same time as Howard, starting a trucking firm in 1936. Initially, Lipe ran routes from South Carolina to Massachusetts, expanding to 65 trucks during World War II. Lipe sold his firm in 1948 and the company went bankrupt two years later.

On a Thursday morning, May 4, 1937, brothers Bill and Holley Cox opened their food store in downtown Hickory. They offered groceries, fresh fruits and vegetables, along with "top quality meats." Bill workedfor another grocer in town before starting his own company with Holley. As the photo shows, the Cox brothers featured delivery services with two trucks prominently displaying their three-digit phone number for call-in orders. In 1948, Bill and Holley expanded offerings to customers under the name Big Dollar Food Market.

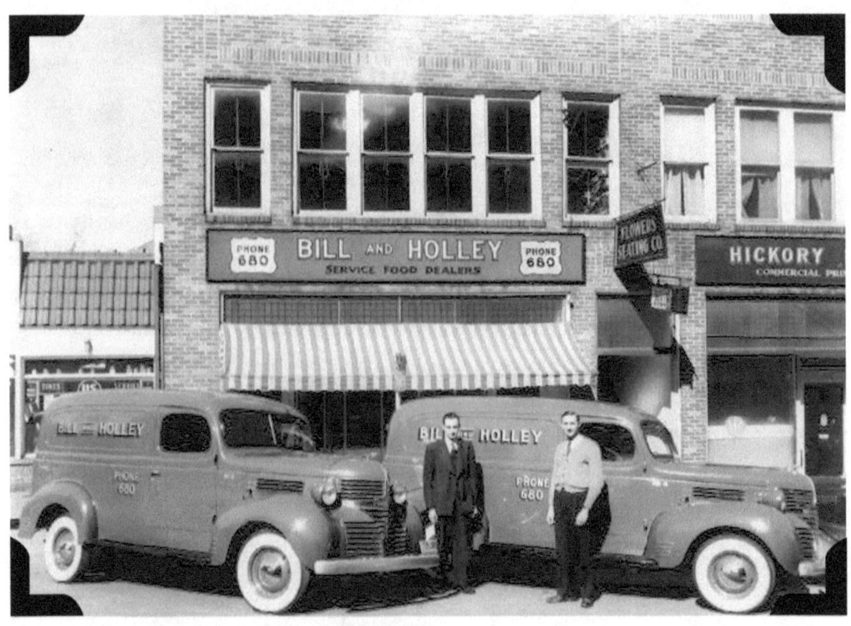

Home of the Hickory Daily Record for 60 years. This colonial styled building may look like a plantation home, but it is actually the third home for the paper that debuted as Hickory's first daily in 1915. Designed by local architectural firm, Clemmer and Horton Associates, all newspaper operations were handled our of this location in downtown Hickory, includ- ing printing the paper.

Union Square, mid-1970s. This image shows the days back when the street ran in front of the buildings, before the square was closed to traffic. Over the years, the flow within Union Square has changed many times but, in the early 1980s, the space directly in front of the storefronts was extend- ed for pedestrian use. Changes occurred in the aftermath of the building of Valley Hills Mall and downtown businesses were suffering. In fact, Butler Shoes, seen in this photo, moved to the mall.

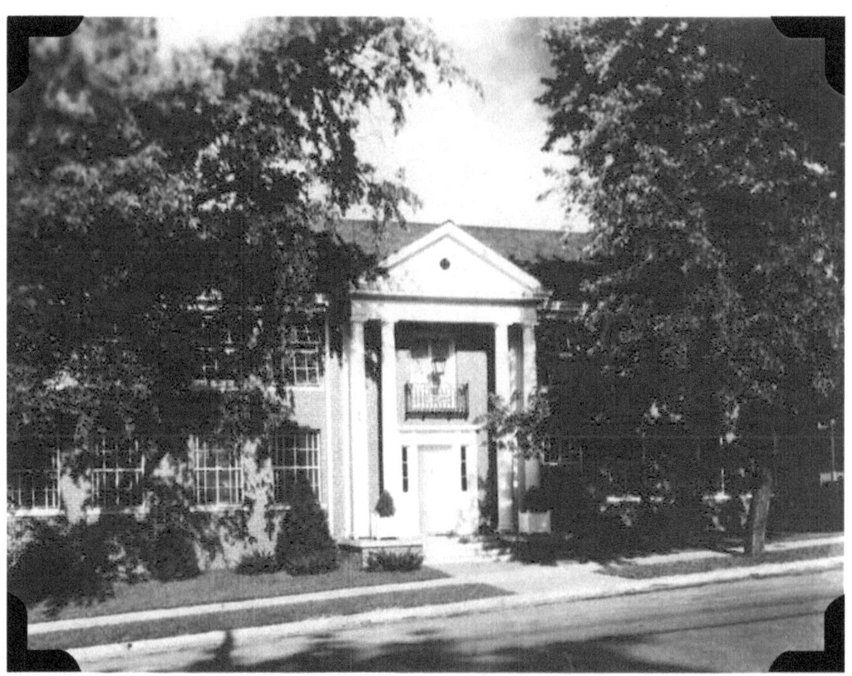

Union Square in the mid-1970s. This photo looks down the block from east to west during the days when a through street ran in front of the line of store fronts. During this period came the rise of enclosed shopping malls on the Highway 70 bypass that lured shoppers away from downtown businesses. Not long after this picture was snapped, Butler Shoes (seen above in the middle of the block) would relocate to Valley Hills Mall. By the early 1980s, the Hickory Downtown Development Association pushed automobile traffic toward the railroad line to give greater room for pedestrian walking space. Note the Square is anchored by Colony Casuals. The women's clothing store held its own fashion show in 1962.

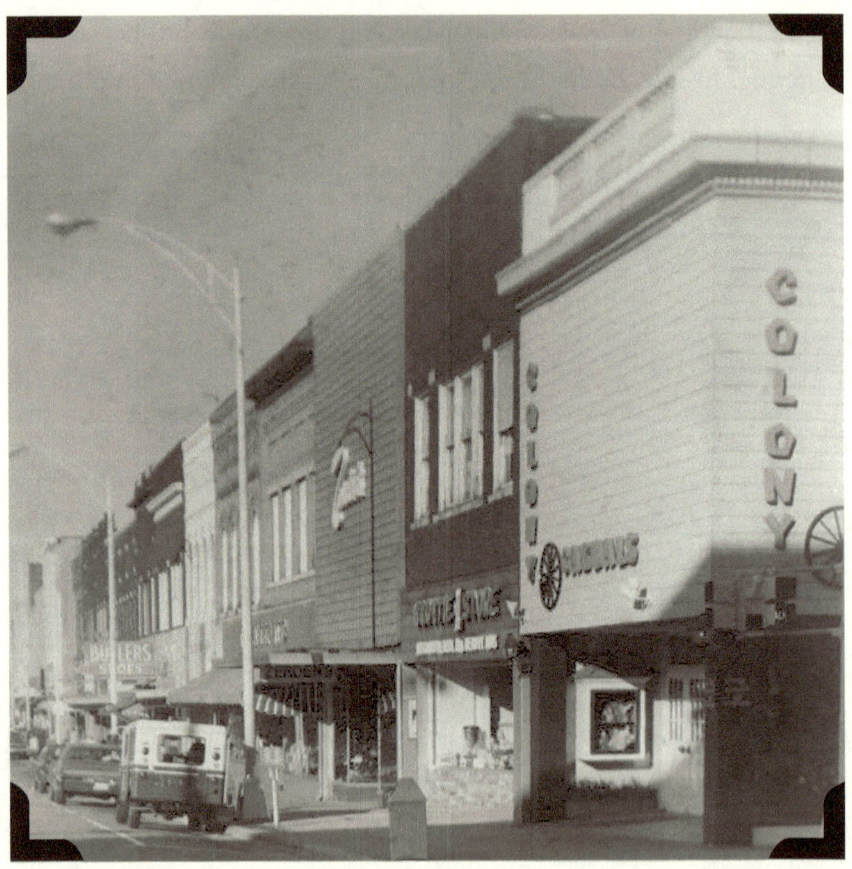

Among the activities for fun among citizens of Catawba County was the fair. Prior to the building of the current Hickory High School, the land in Viewmont was home to annual event. These two unidentified ferris wheel riders look to be enjoying themselves, as were many attendees who bought their ticket and felt the vicarious thrills of weightlessness each time the wheel spun around.

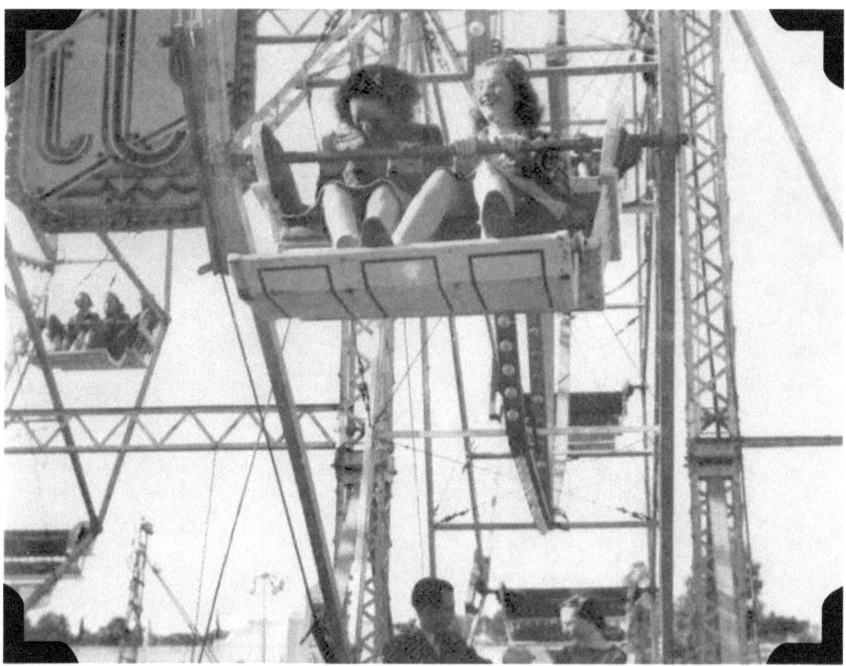

CHAPTER 4

FACES

One of the ways C.M. Hardin kept his photographic studio profitable was to go to family reunions and take images of the clan. The image below serves as an example. This unidentified family assembled near the Catawba County town of Claremont to renew family ties, enjoy a meal together and have their likeness taken for posterity. The organization of the photo is typical with the children sitting down front, a row sitting with chairs brought from inside and the rest standing.

Throughout the rest of the chapter are images of people who sat for their portraits to be taken by the Hardin lens. Some are identified, some not. Occasionally, the briefest of explanations are given for why the image was needed, as in used for a passport. Otherwise, the reason for capturing their likeness remained known only to them.

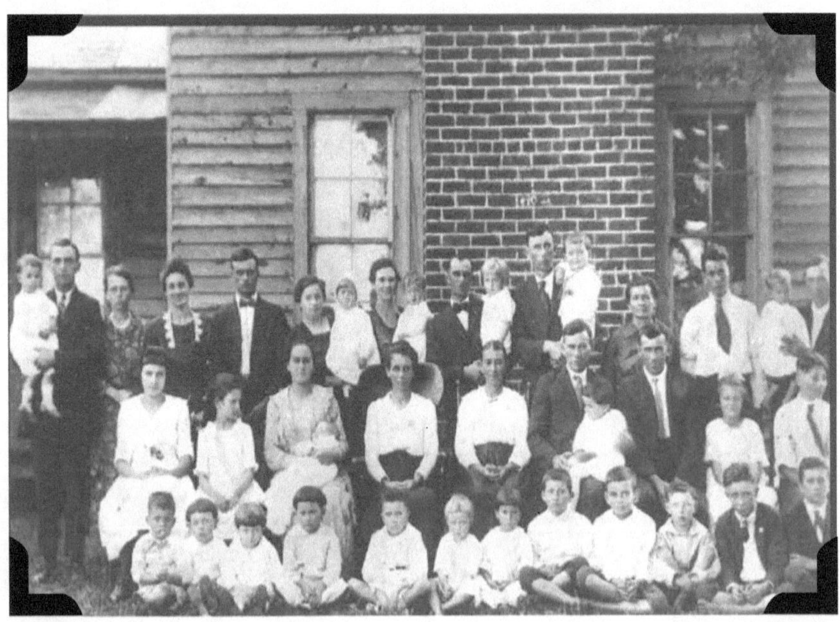

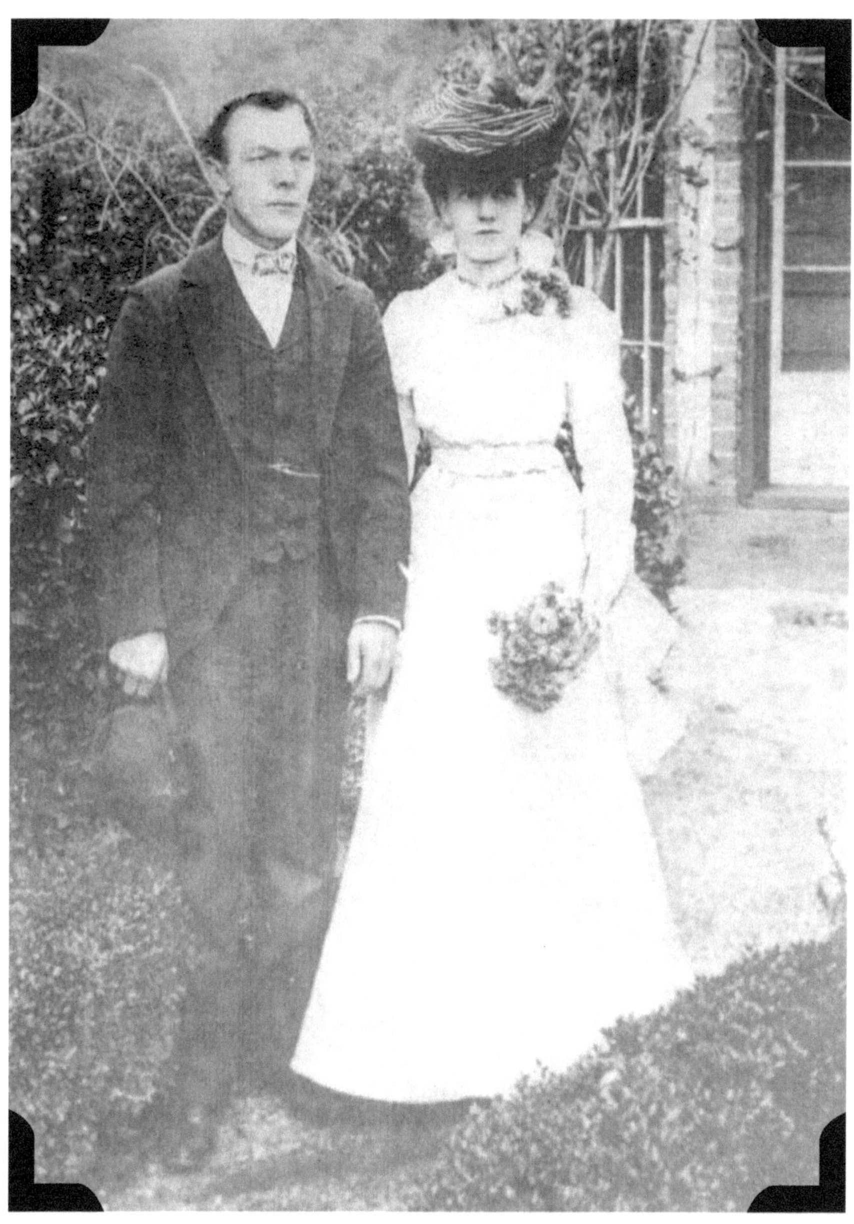

A bride and groom.

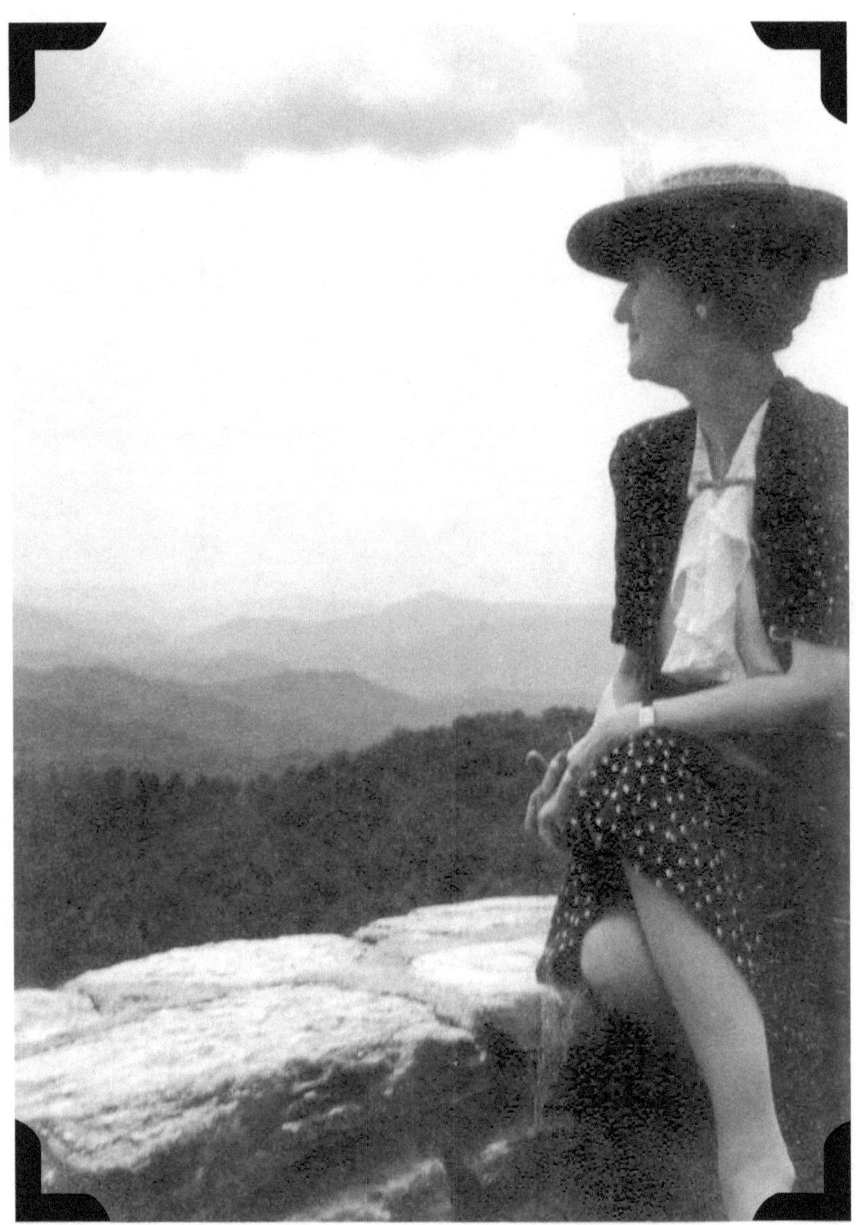

Mrs. Elbert Lyerly

Taken by Kathryn Hardin Whitner

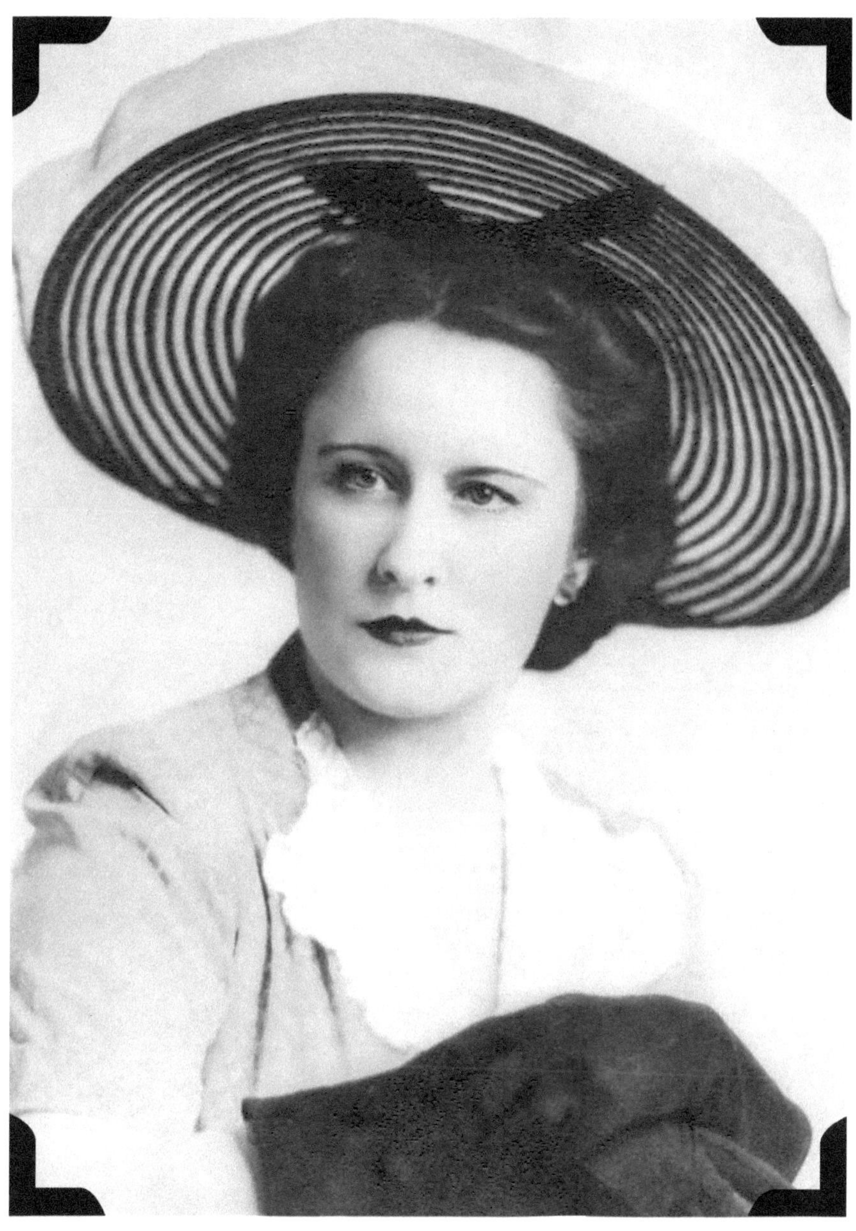

Carolyn Nichols Brawley

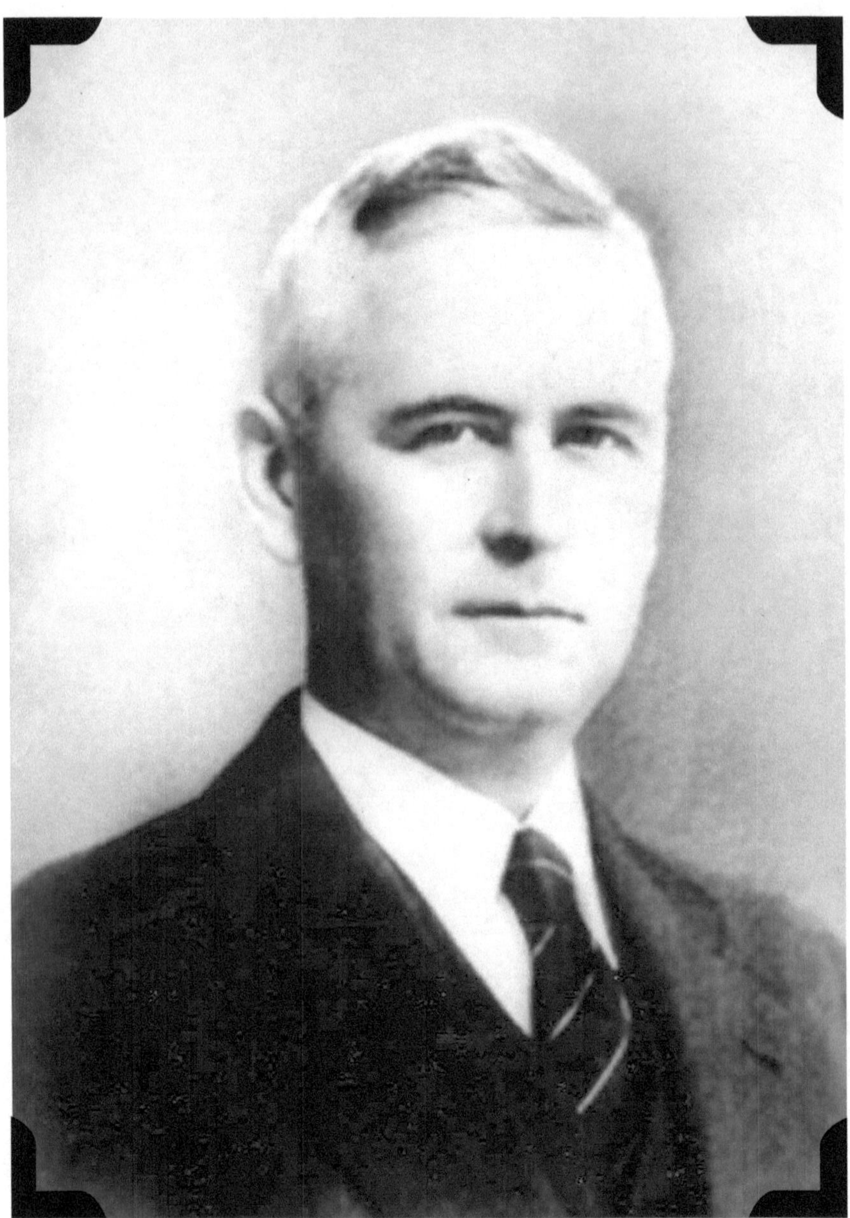

Dr. John Hay

Mary Lipe, also known as Mrs. Carl V. Cline, Sr.

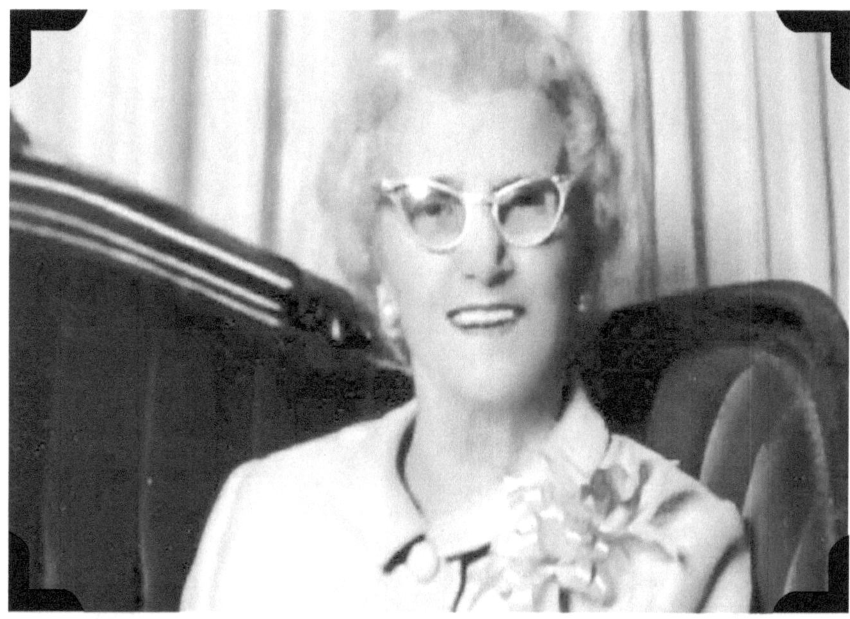

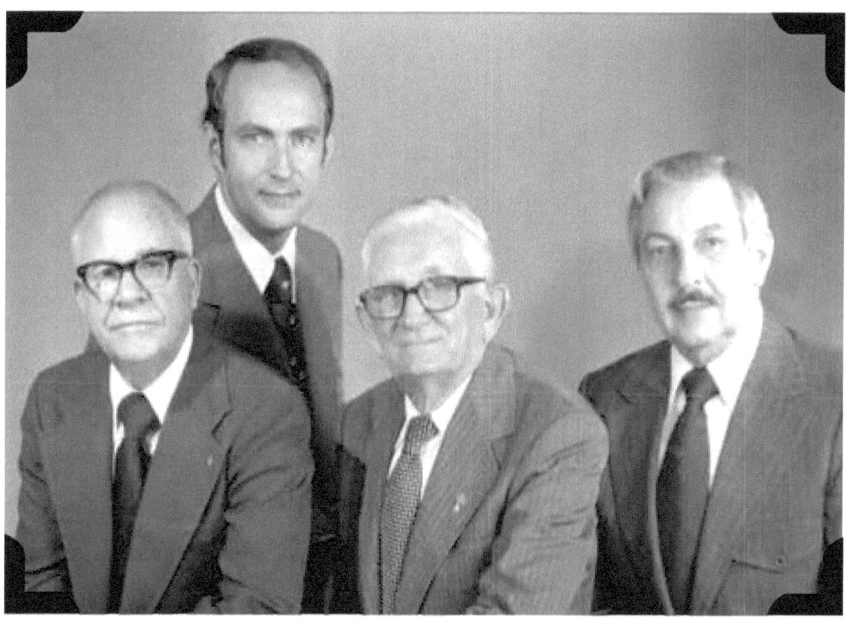

A group of Hickory Professionals that included Bob Clemmons.

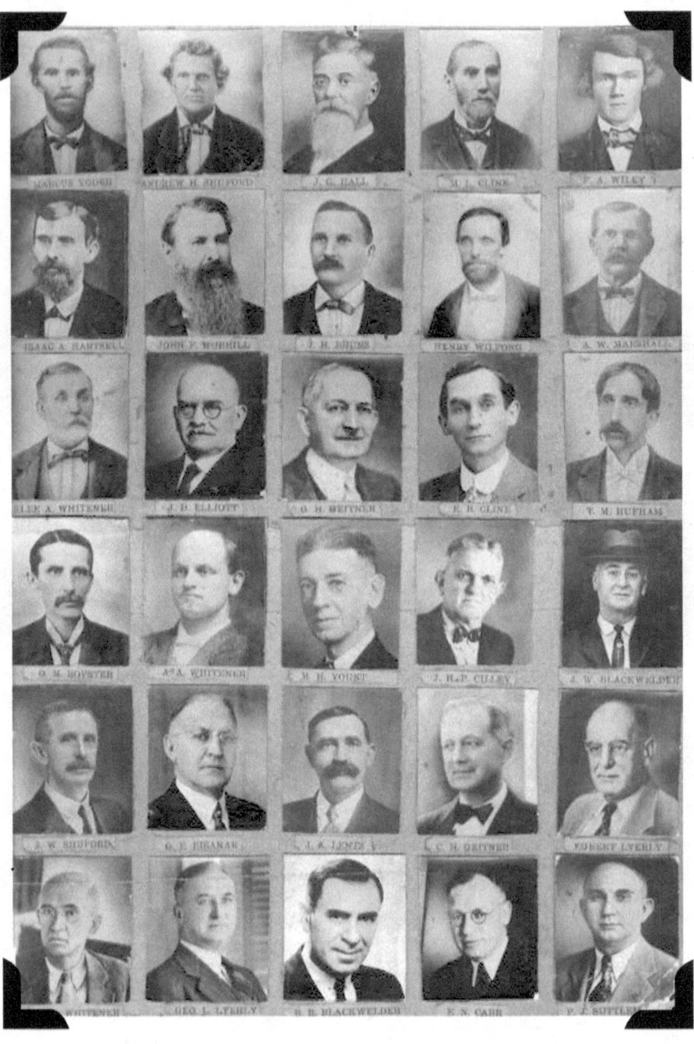

The mayors of Hickory. The portraits taken prior to 1900 were done by other photographers, but once C.M. arrived he took his place as profes- sional known for capturing the best possible image of his subject and was sought after for his skill behind the camera. The reputation of the Hardin studio lived beyond C.M.'s passing in 1941 with Kathryn taking over. She employed the same skills as her father, helping Hickory's mayors to look as dignified as possible.

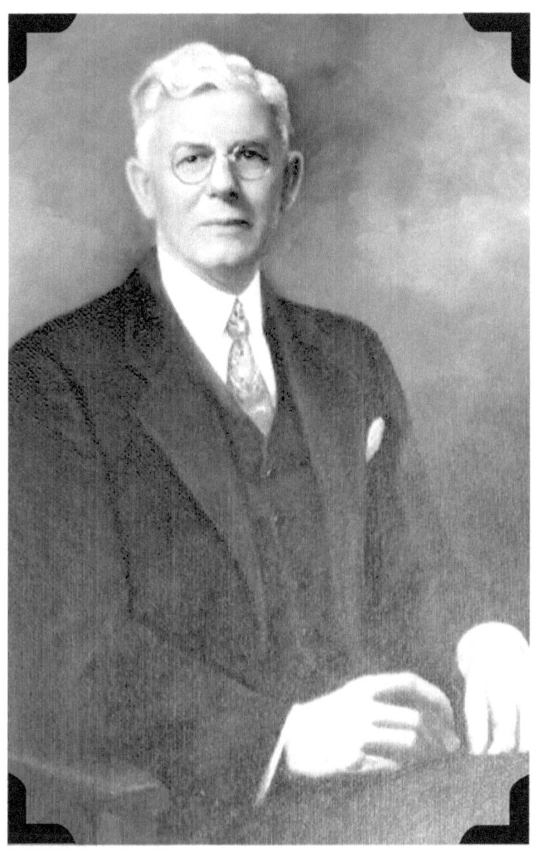

George W. Hall, the father of the furniture industry in Hickory. According to lore, Hall was standing in his family's store on Union Square, watching a train pass hauling lumber. Some say a mishap had caused planks to fall from the flat cars on which they had been loaded. Whatever the circumstance, he thought of how that lumber might wind up in the furniture making capital of the United States then (Grand Rapids, Michigan), be honed into dressers, bedsteads and other household pieces and then return to Hickory as finished pieces, denying his hometown to miss out on the value added to the wood in making furniture. He worked to bring capital together to establish Hickory Manufacturing in 1901, the town's first home furnishings factory.

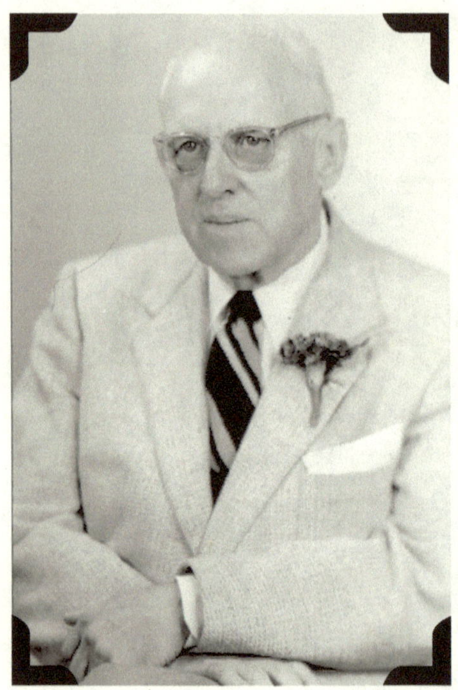

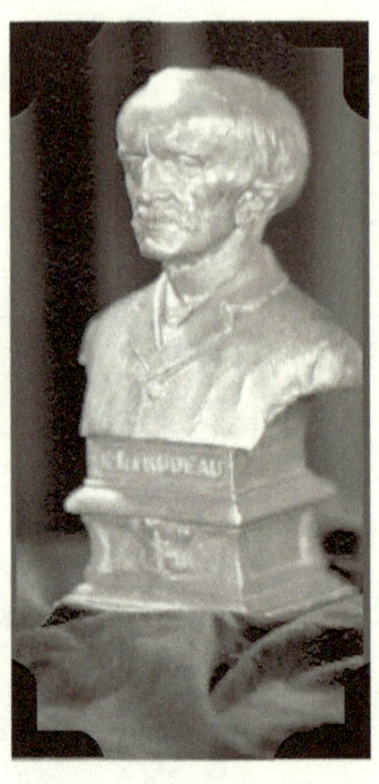

Dr. Gaither Hawn, a Hickory physician. During the polio epidemic of 1944, Dr. Hawn was part of a core group of medical professionals who determined the need for an emergency hospital in Hickory. They converted a city building that ultimate treated 454 patients, diagnosed with po- lio. The success rate of the hos- pital was over 97%. In the years after the epidemic, Dr. Hawn was known to driver former sufferers of the disease to Gastonia for corrective surgery at his own expense. This photograph of Dr. Hawn was taken in 1955. The bust is of Dr. Edward Livingston Trudeau, whose institute, on Saranac Lake in New York assisted respiratory patients. Dr. Hawn was a patient there, recovering from WWI injuries and studied there, which helped in his understanding of polio. It is likely that the photograph of Dr. Trudeau was commissioned by Dr. Hawn.

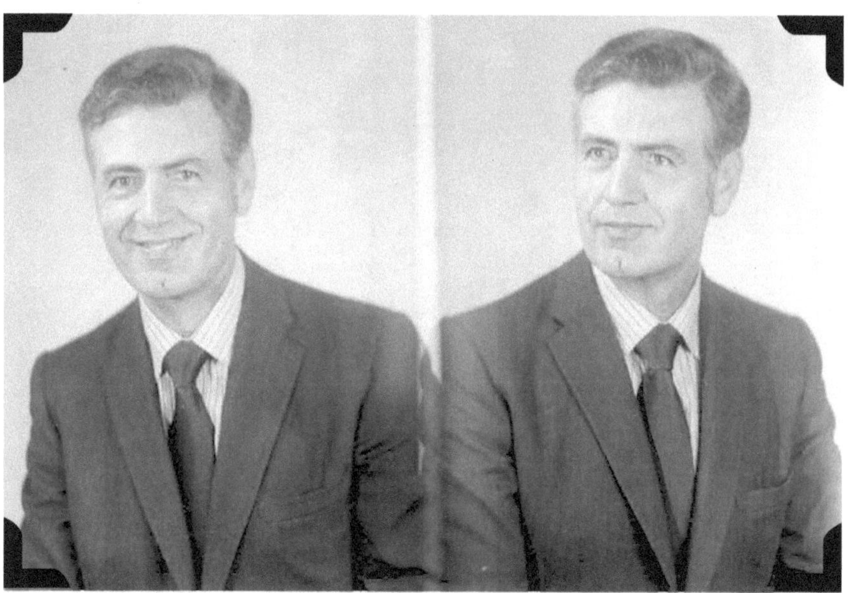

Shots of Angelo Emanuel, owner of Angelo's Shoes, a longtime downtown Hickory business.

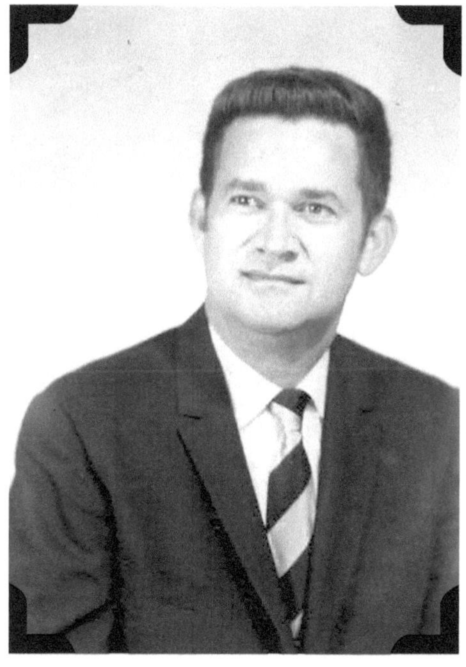

Albert Allran worked in the textile industry, ultimately becoming part owner of Maiden Mills. He was a decorated veteran of World War II and served his community on numerous boards and councils, but perhaps themost significant contribution was his tenure as president of Lenoir-Rhyne College. He guided the college through a difficult transitionary period in the 1980s, helping the college to return to a stable financial footing.

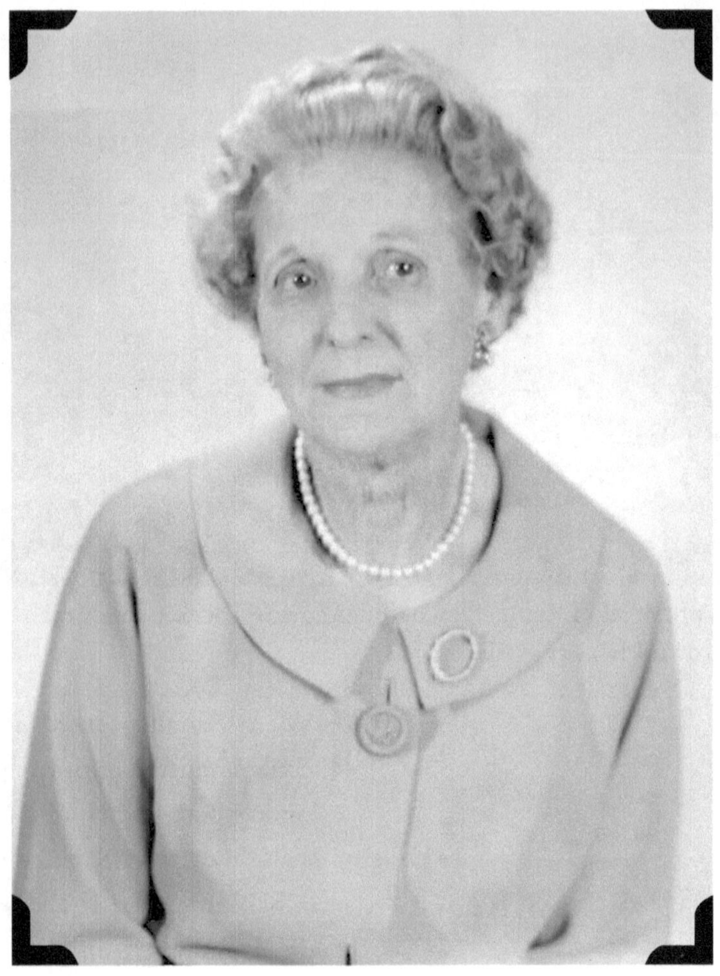

Mabel Miller Rowe was a driving force in establishing the Hickory Daily Record. She and her brother Carl "Red" Miller, started the paper in 1915, leaving college to serve as the paper's first reporter. In the newsroom, everyone knew her as Miss Mabel. When the paper was sold, she stayed on as society editor. When she passed away in 1979, one tribute said, "newspapering at the Record with the possible exception of Mabel Miller Rowe was a man's world."

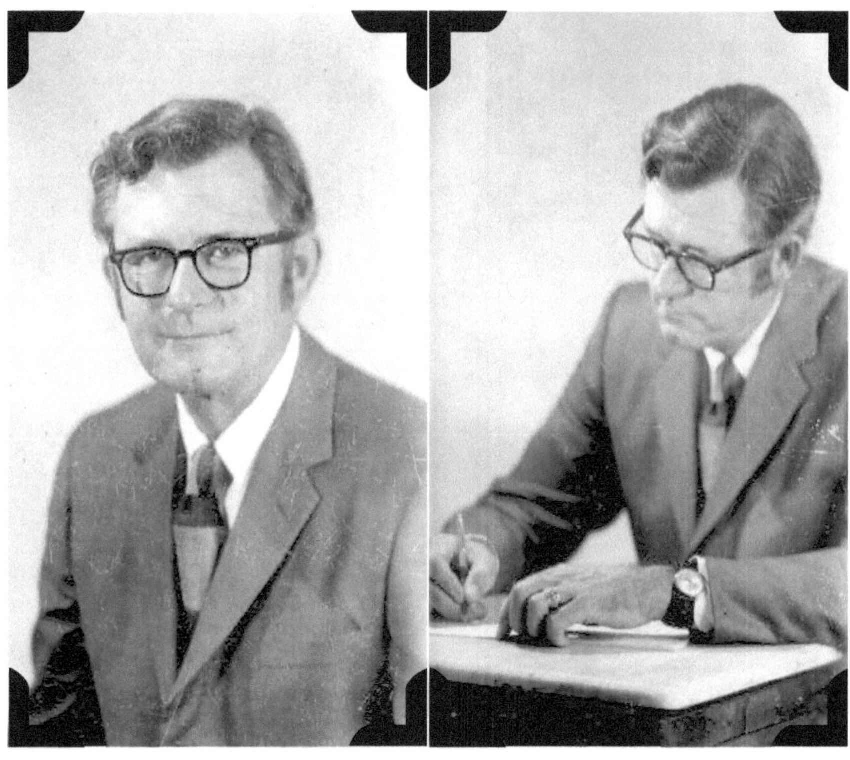

A musician, aviator and architect, Beemer Harrell posed for Kathryn's camera in 1971. A native of Monroe, NC, he moved to Hickory in 1950 with two degrees in architecture. Through his firm, he designed numer- ous buildings including some of the city's most unique homes. Harrell was a Renaissance man, the author of two books, he helped found the Hickory Downtown Development Association and the city's Oktoberfest celebration.

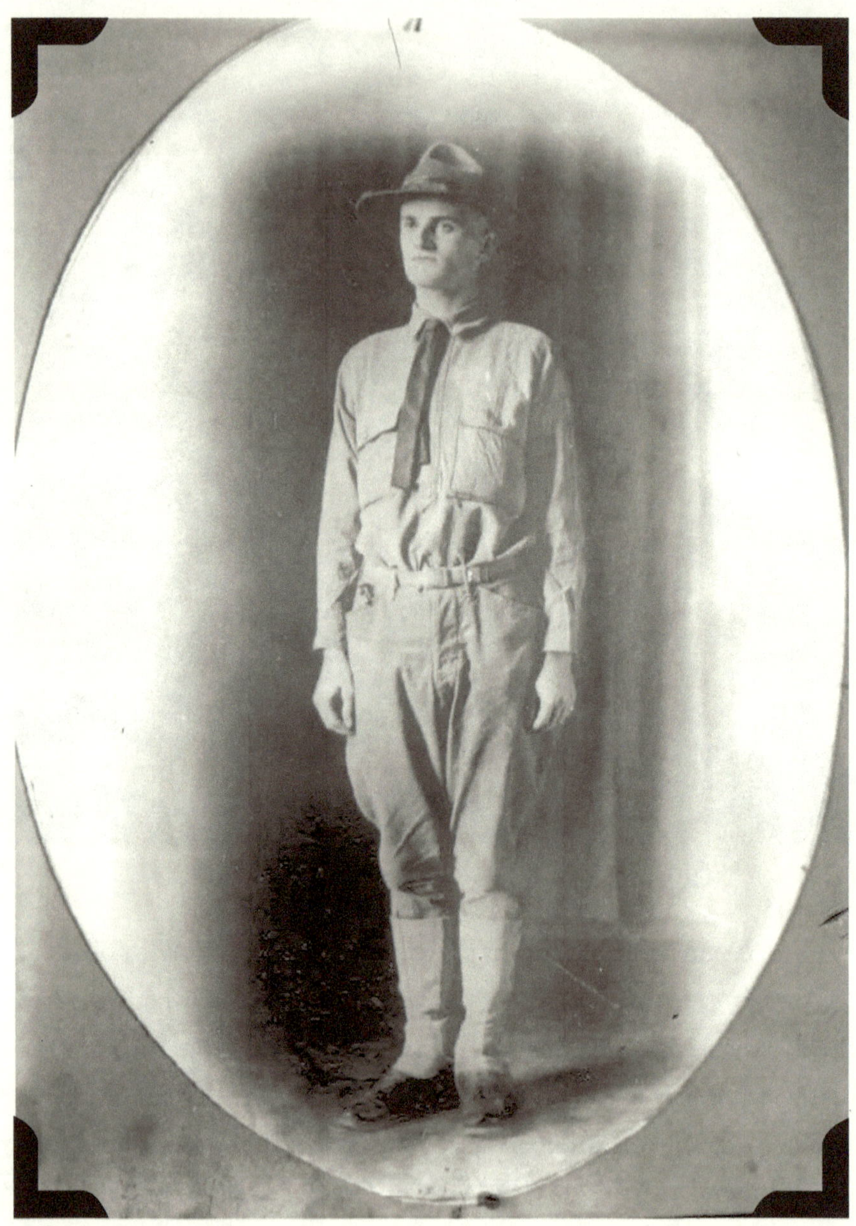

An unknown soldier.

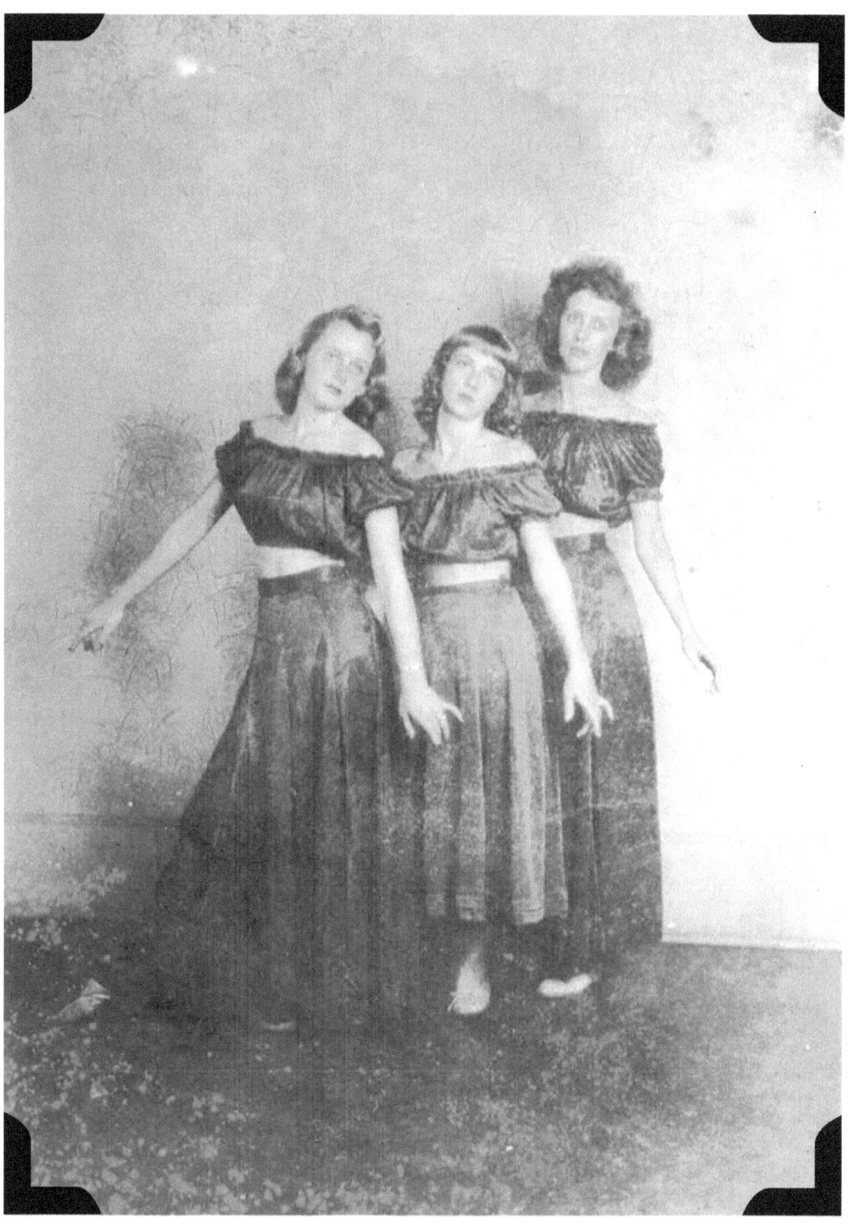

Dancers

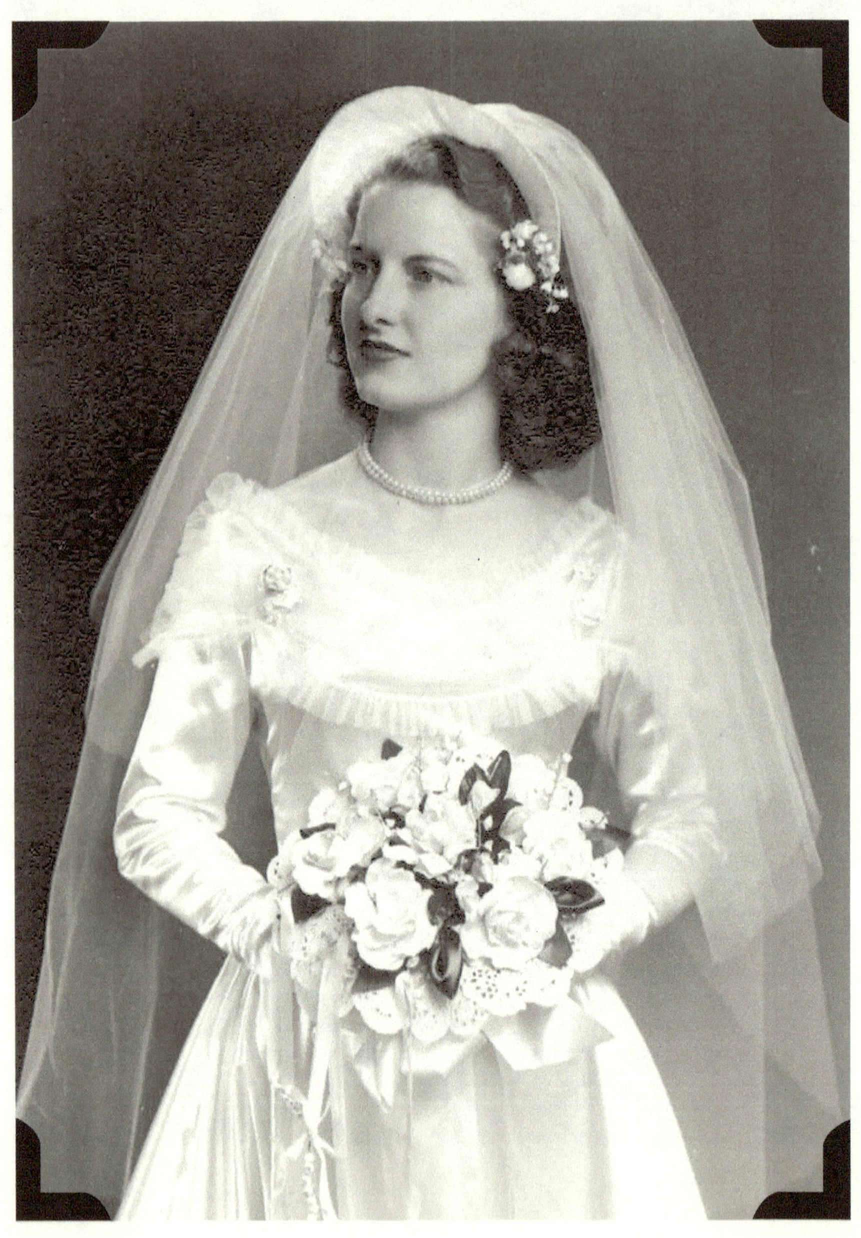

CHAPTER 5

THE SPECIAL DAY

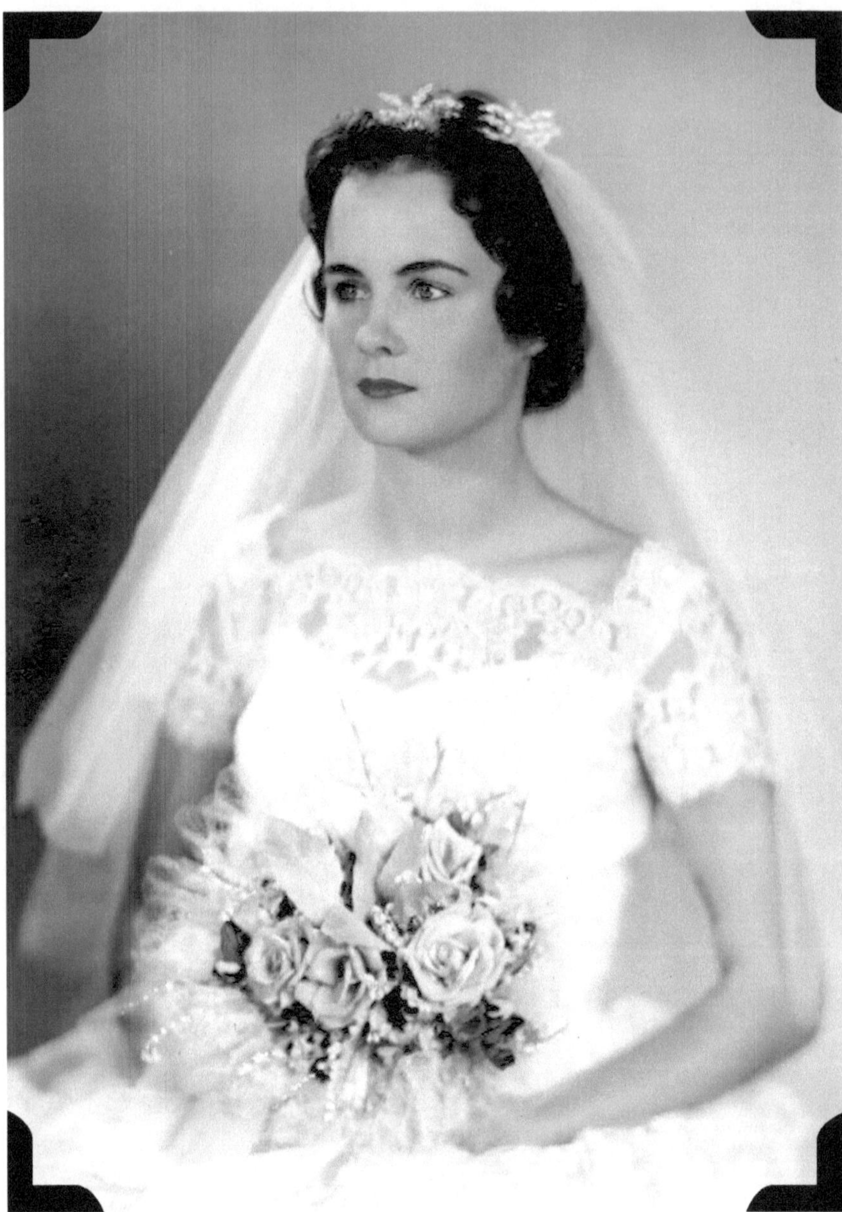

Among noteworthy days, perhaps a wedding tops the list as the most documented. A sample of some of the bridal photography done by the Hardin Studio, show subjects selecting images of themselves in poses that range from thoughtful to statuesque, all with a hopeful countenance.

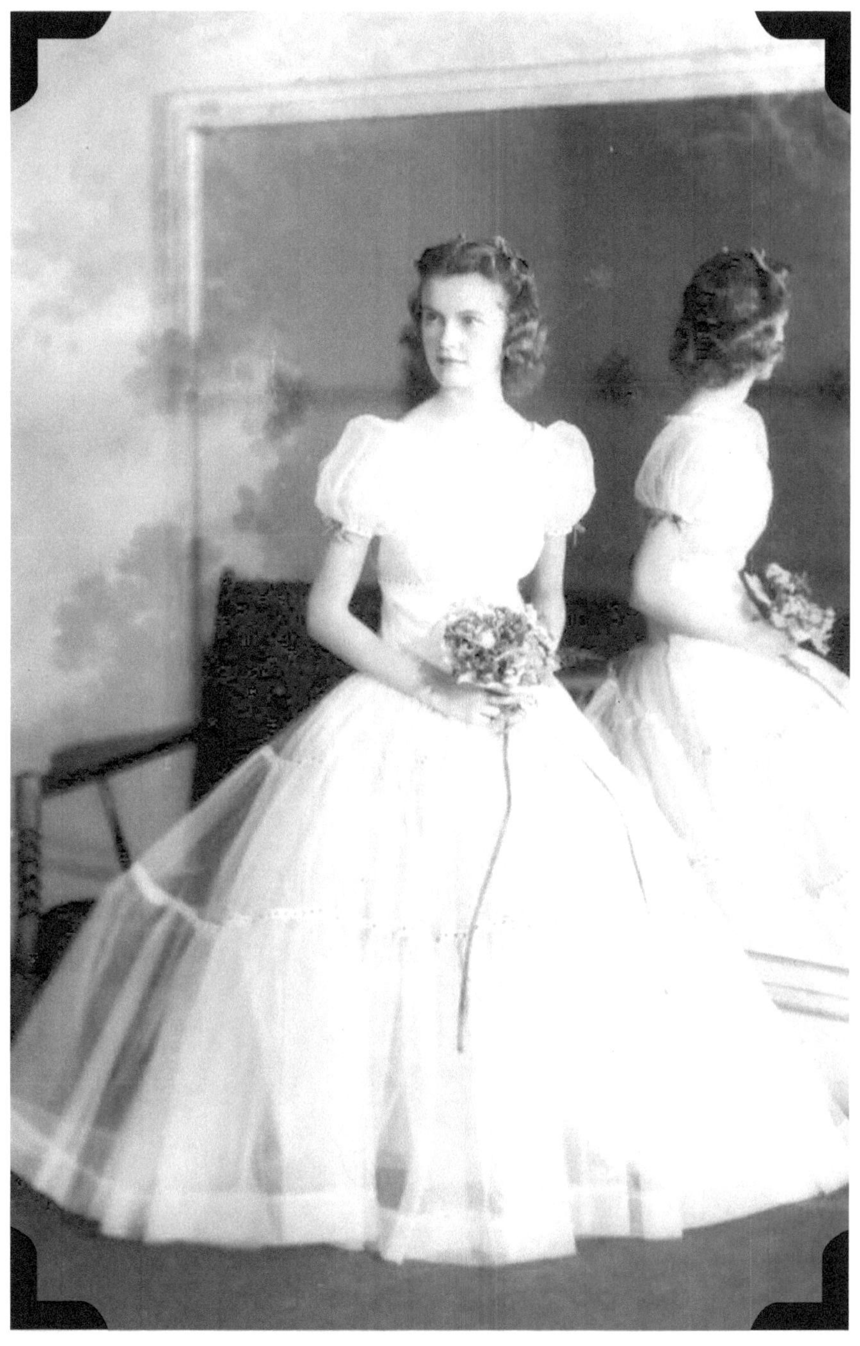

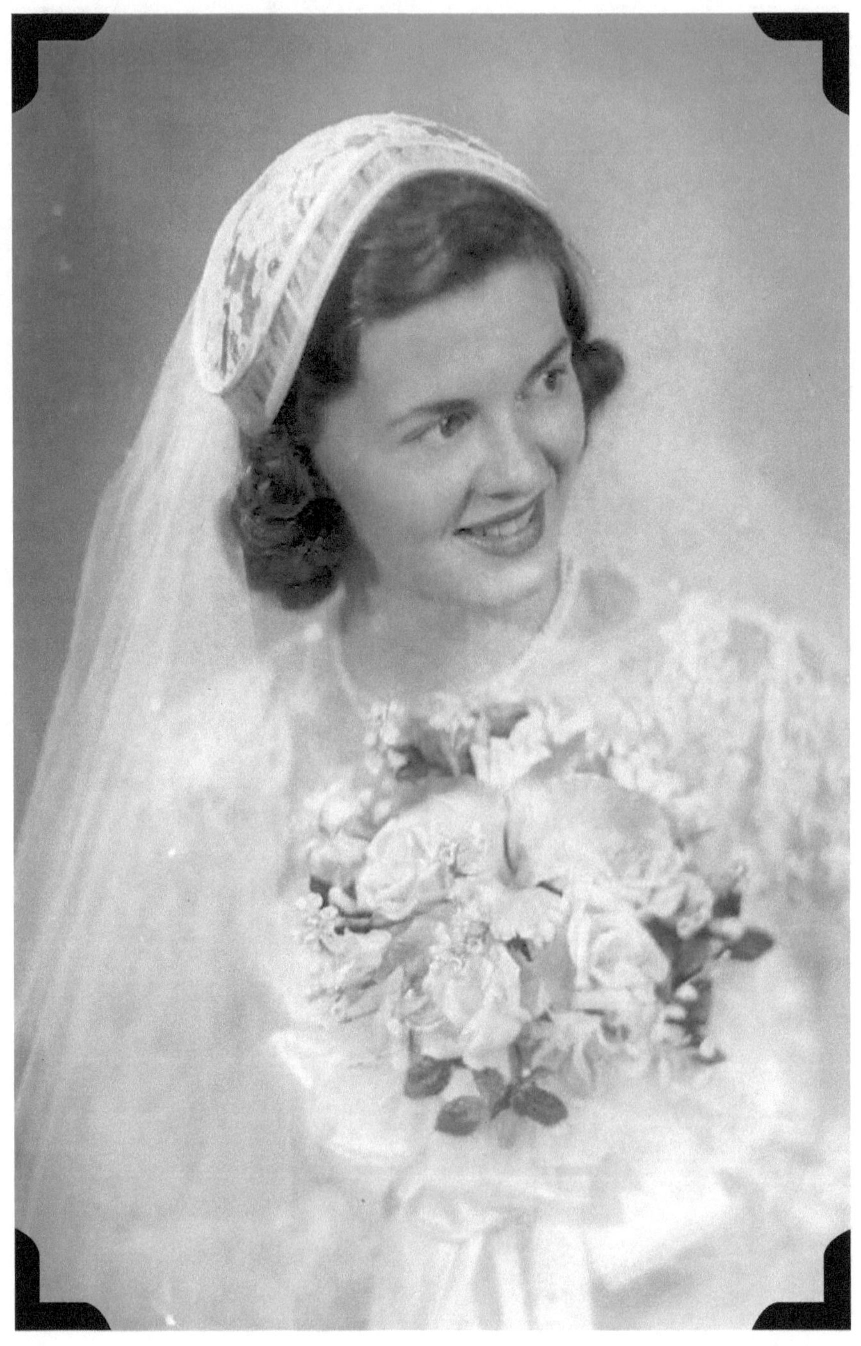

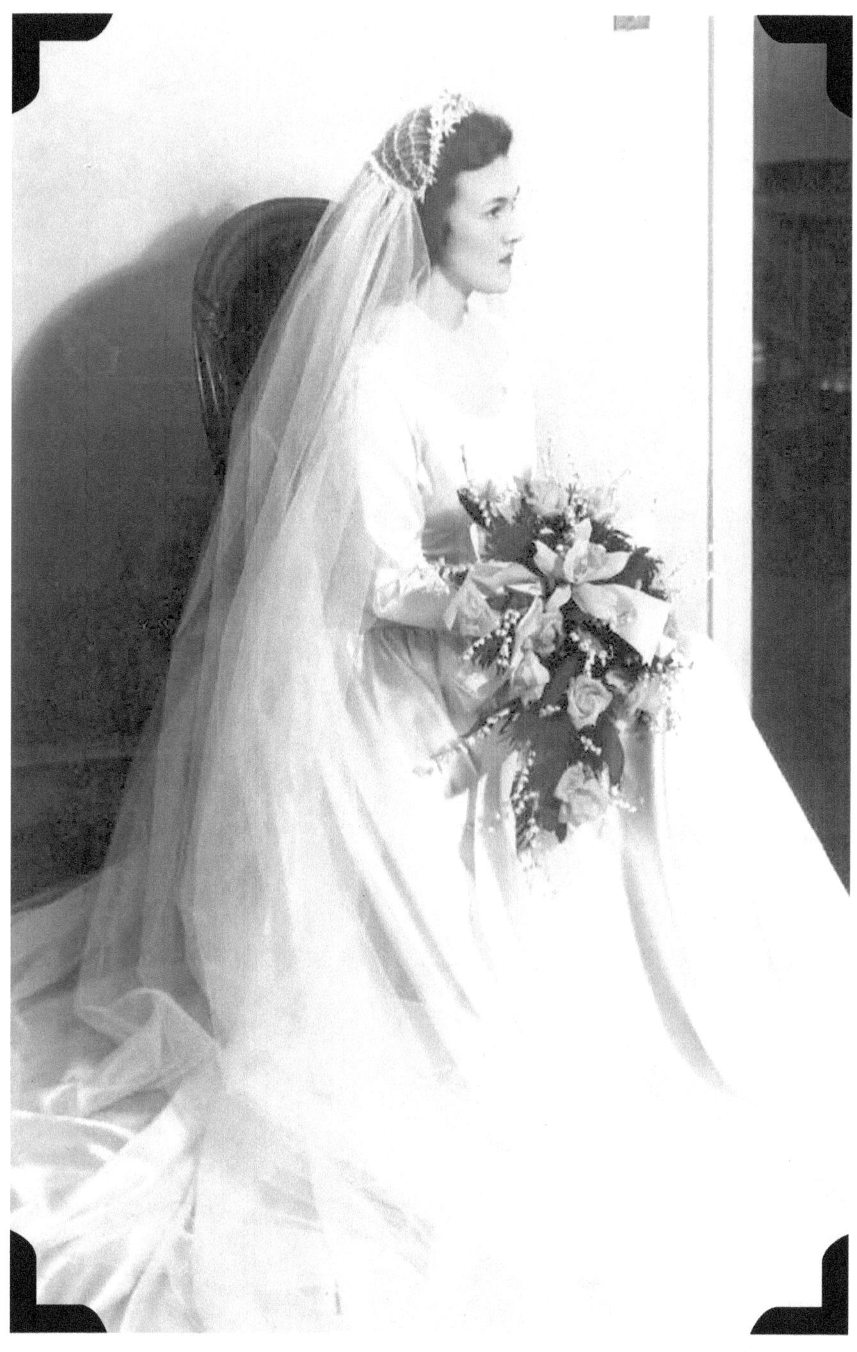

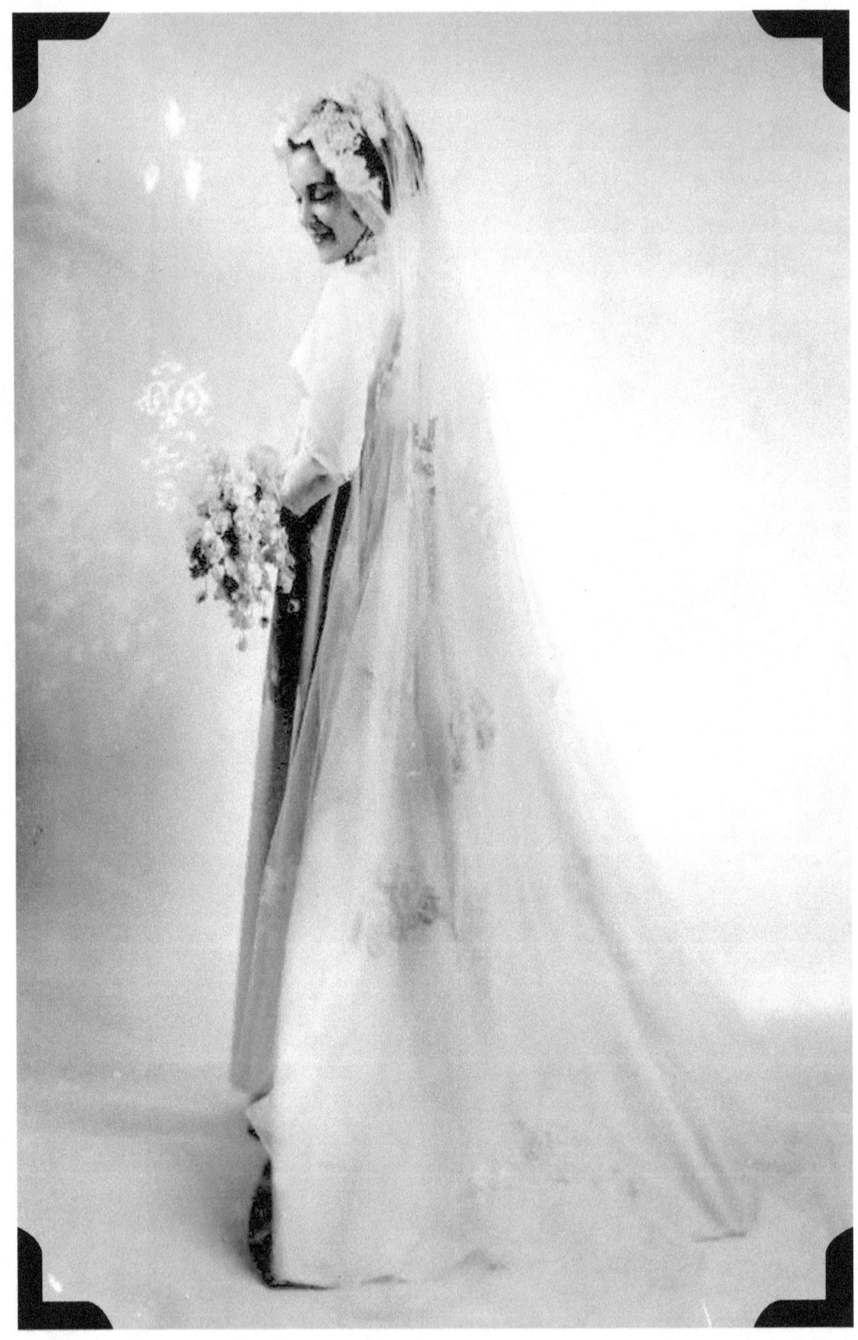

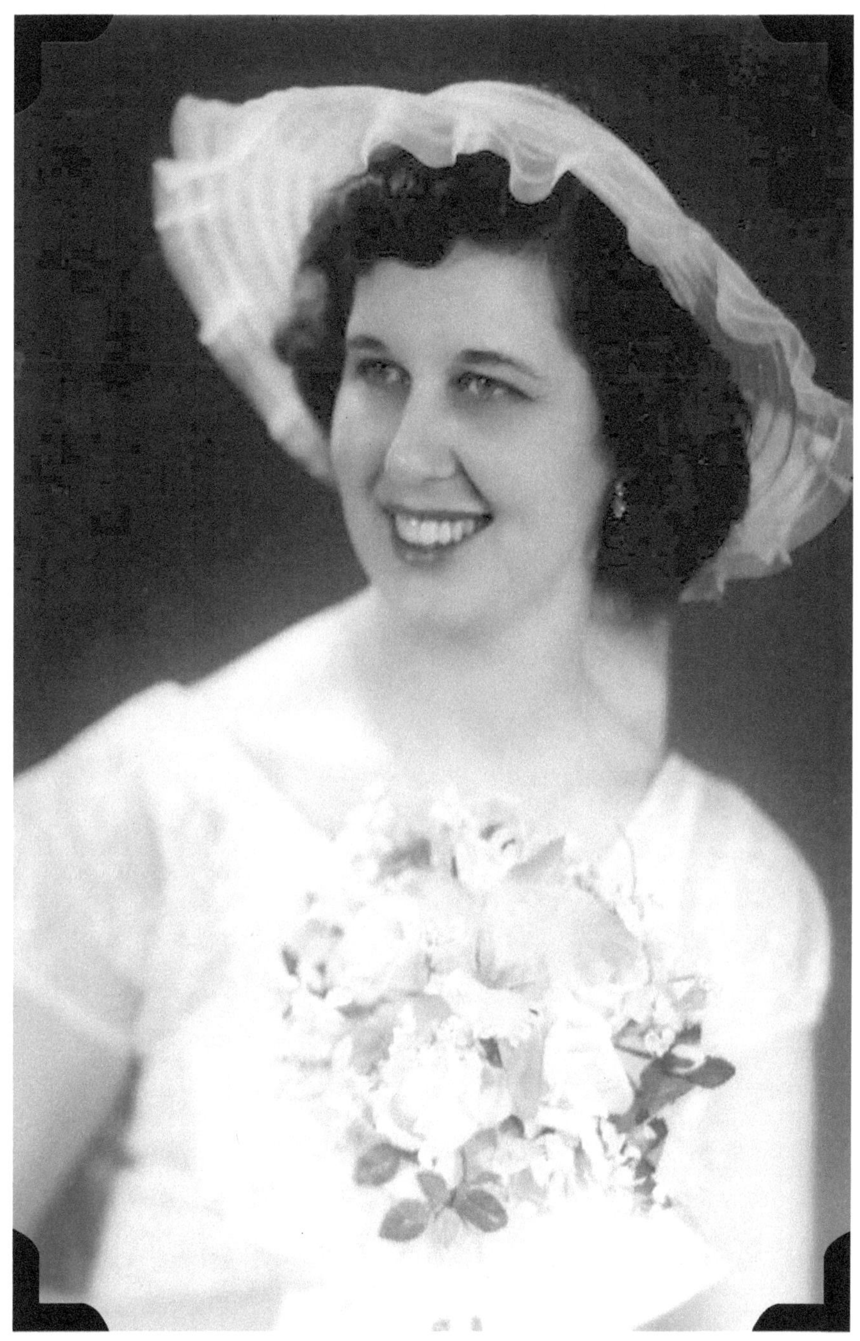

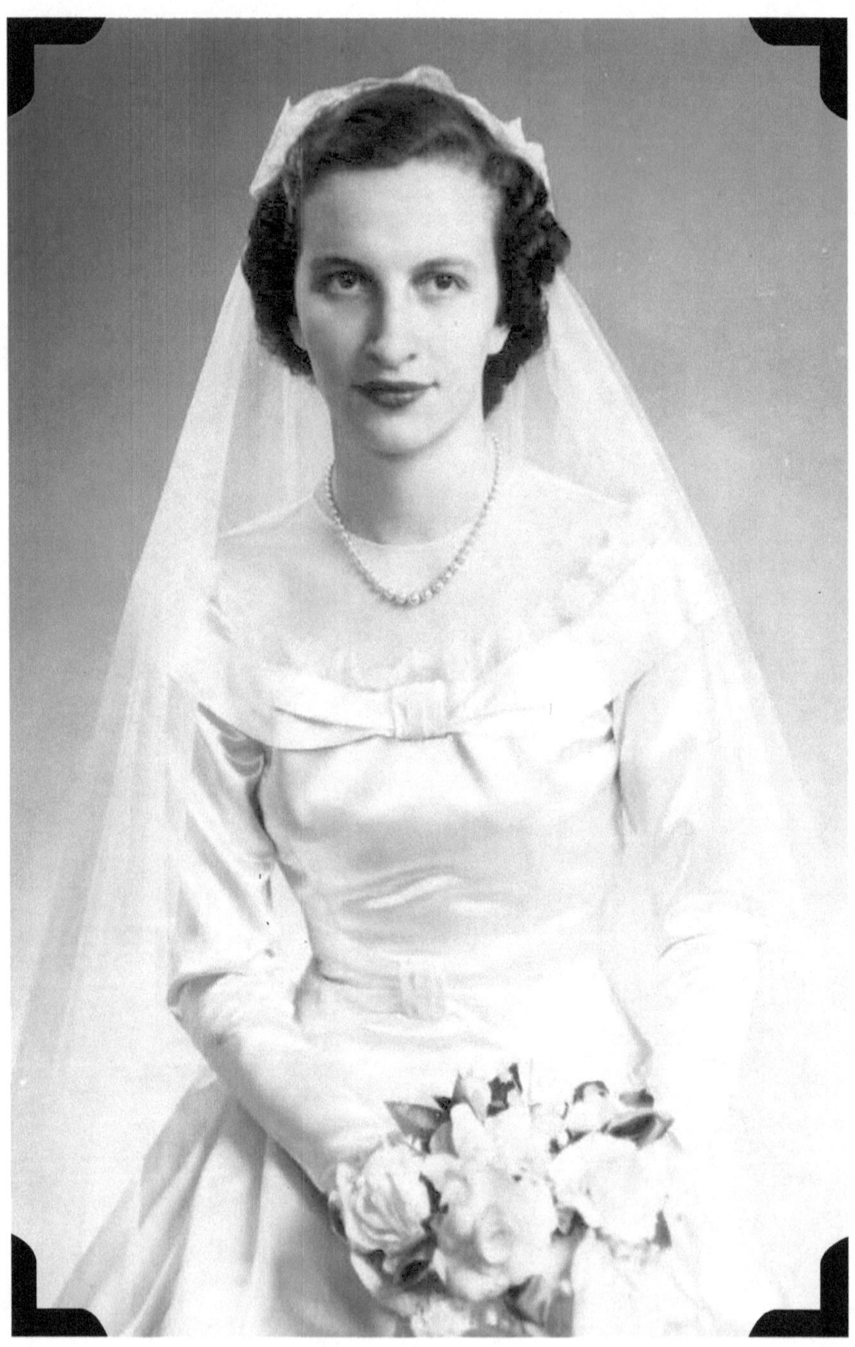

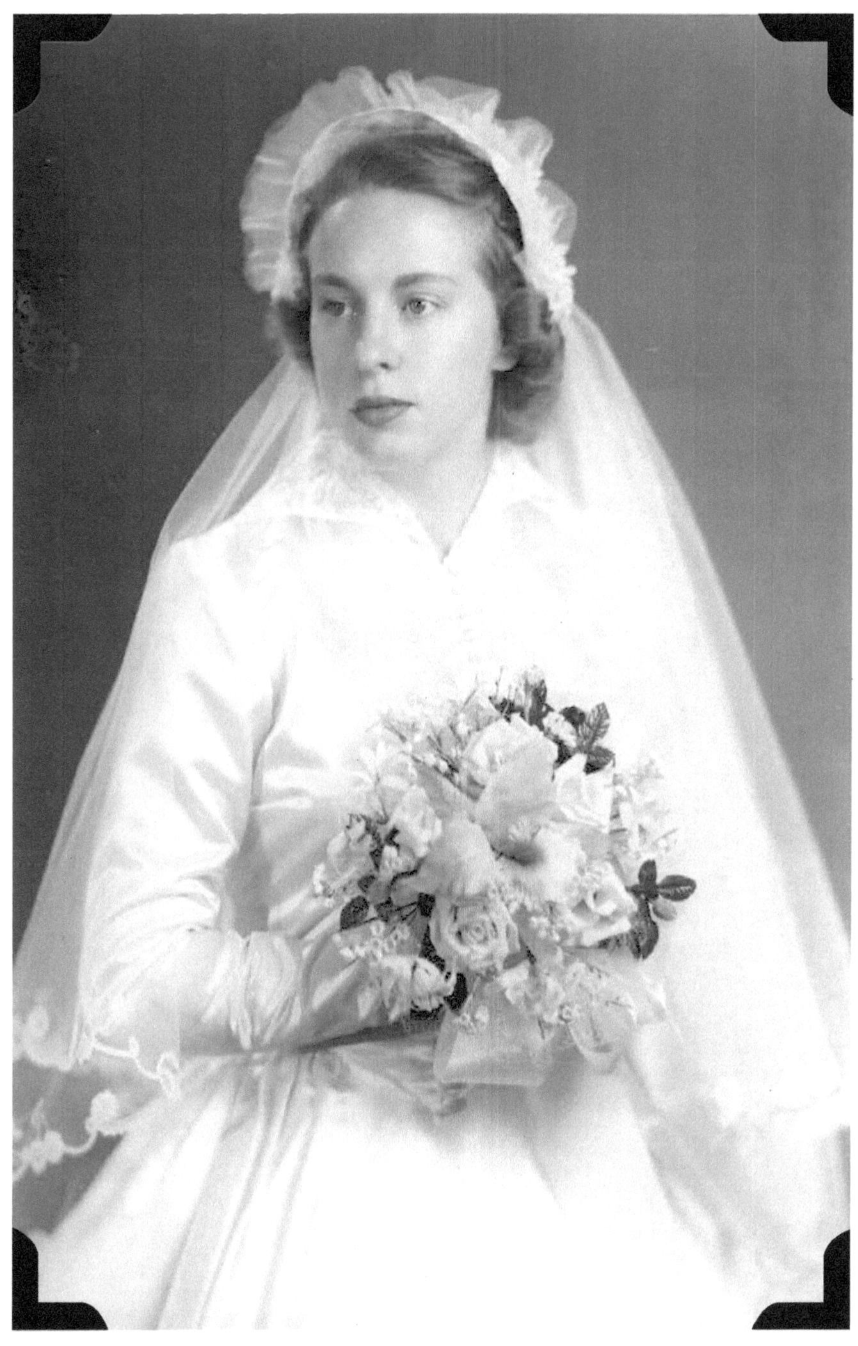

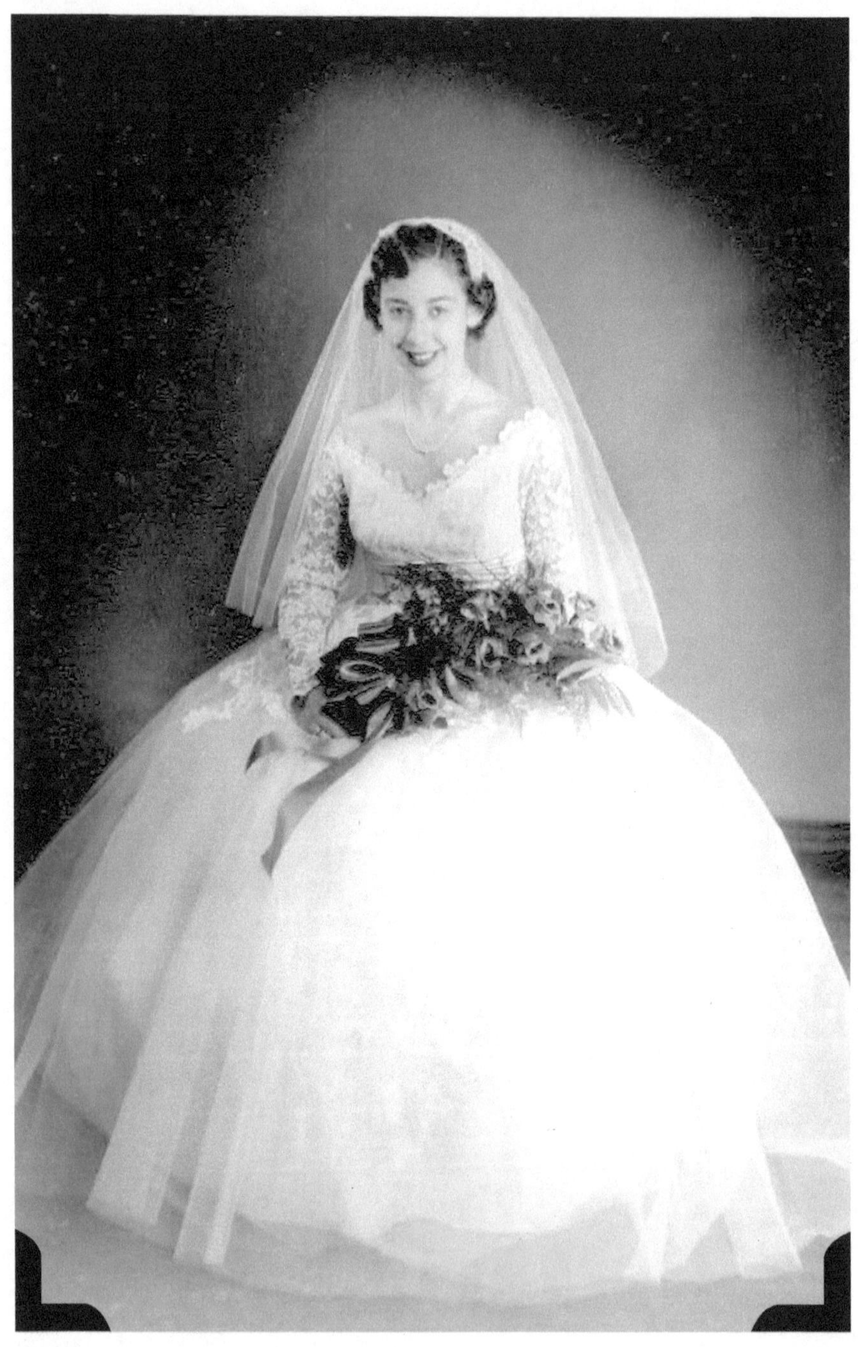

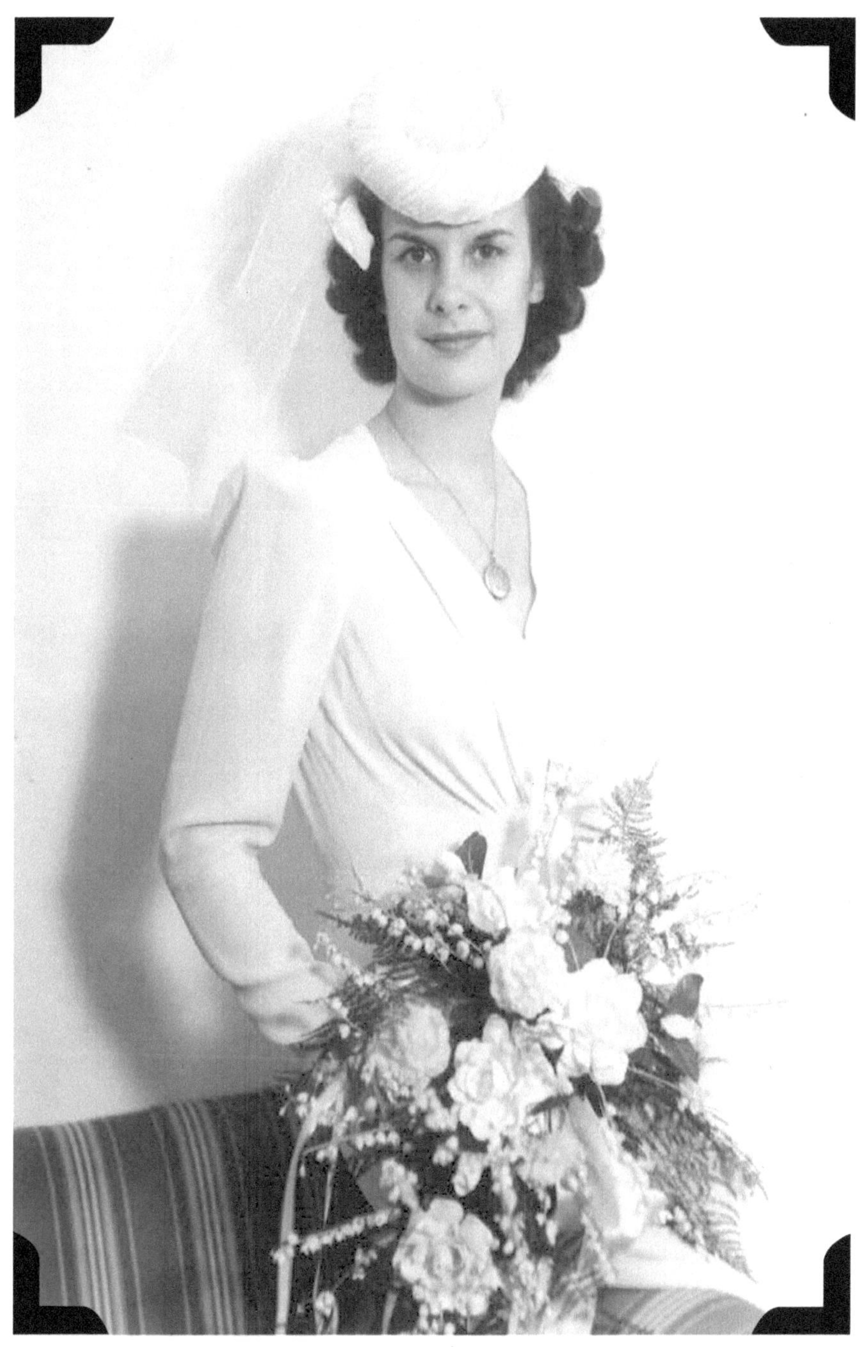

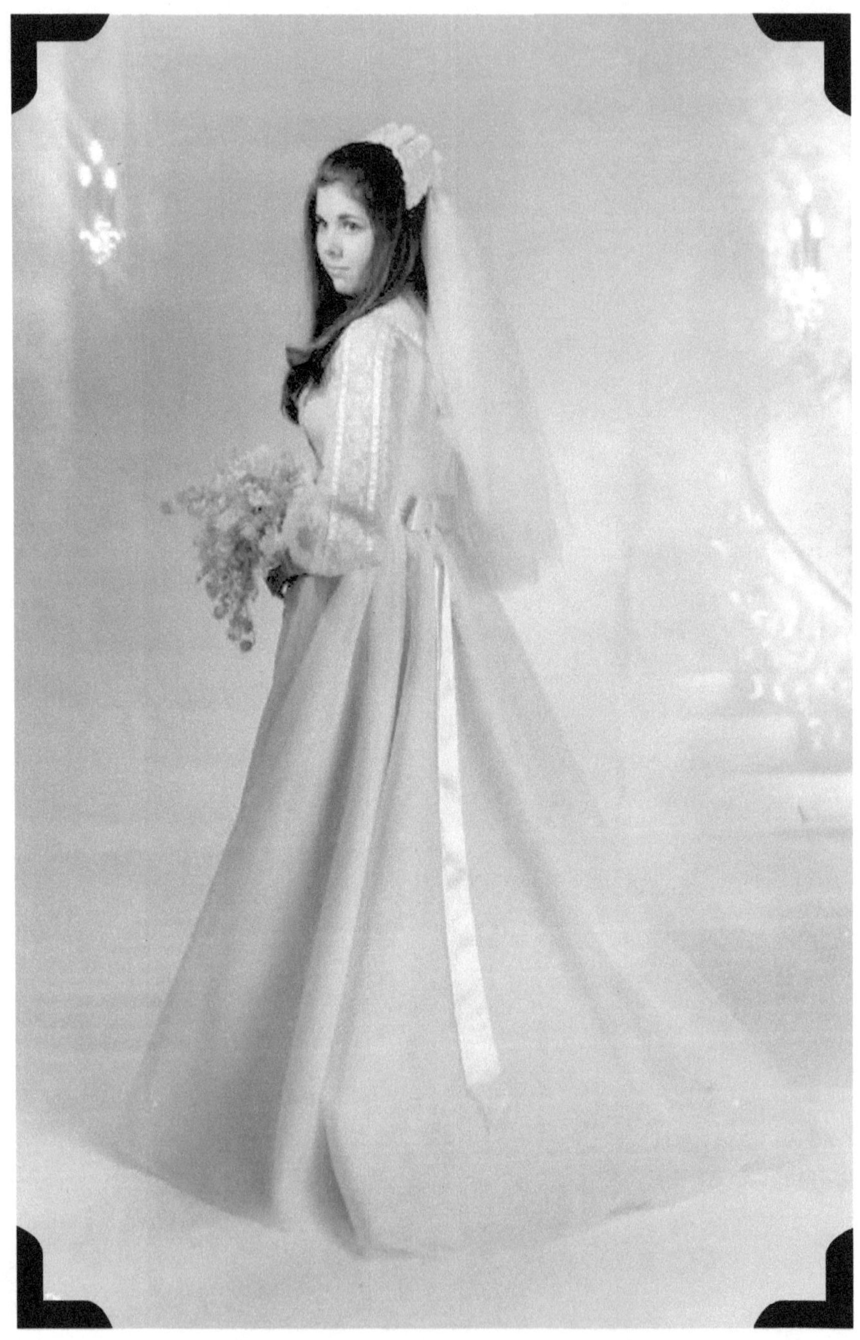

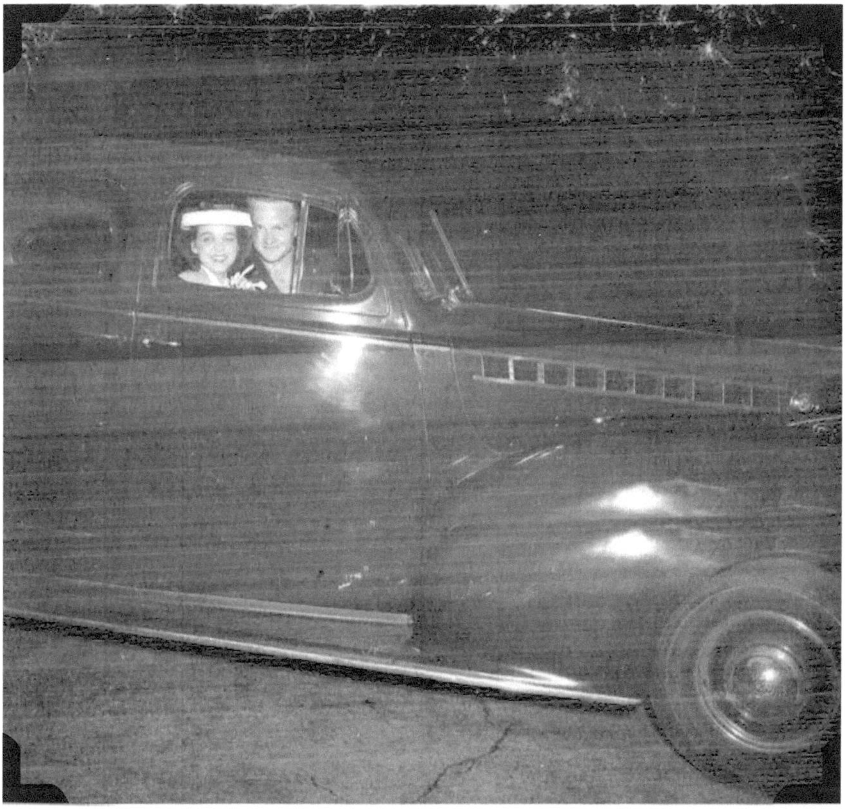

This last shot was of more personal concern to Kathryn. Her daughter, Peggy Stewart Whitener married Flight Officer Benjamin Goodman in Hickory on May 12, 1945. This picture, photographer unknown, snapped the image as the newly married couple were leaving for their honeymoon after a ceremony at First Baptist and a reception.

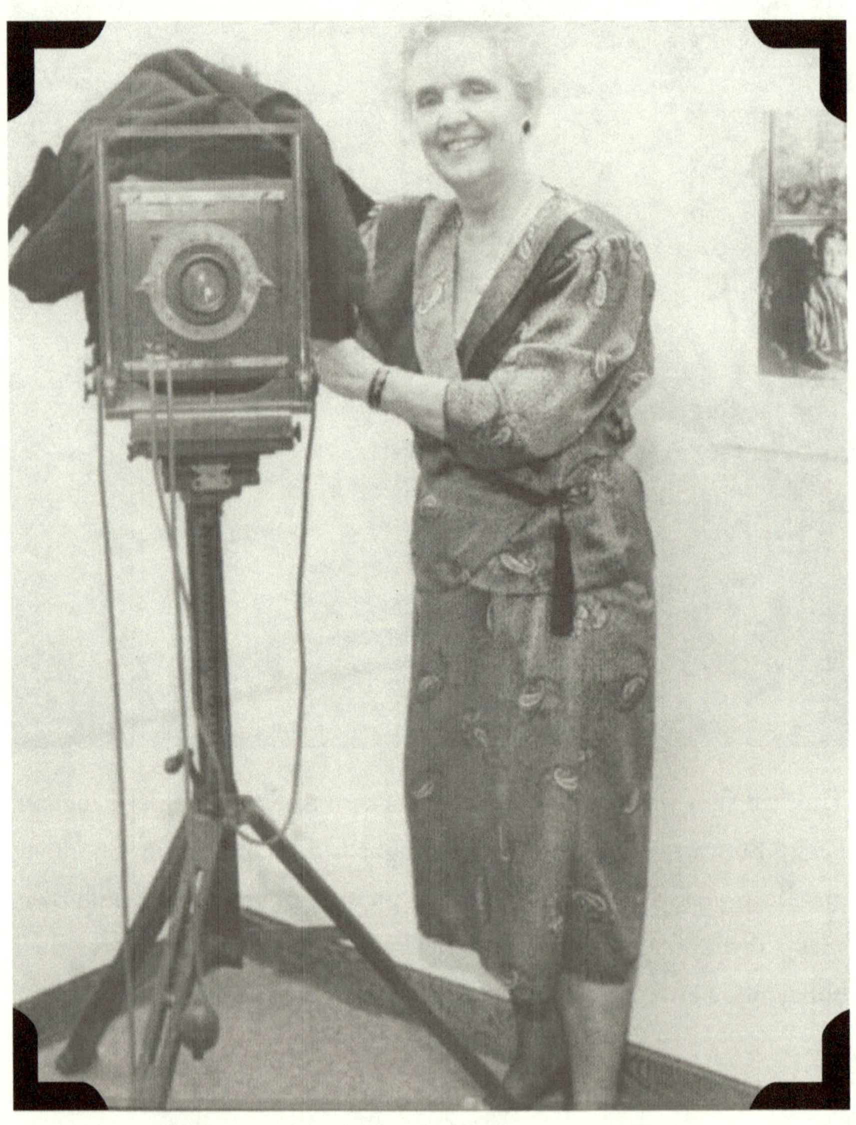

Peggy Goodman and the family camera.

CHAPTER 6

REFLECTING ON A LEGACY OF IMAGES

For most of the twentieth century, the Hardin family tradition of photographing Hickory offers a look at what people cherished as keepsakes. C.M. Hardin and/or his daughter Kathryn Hardin Whitener snapped images of hundreds, if not thousands of faces in town to preserve the moment. Much of what went through the Hardin lens documents the life of a growing, prosperous population that set the stage for the city of today.

Many of the images that snapped into existence from the Hardin studio are now part of the Hickory Museum of Art's permanent collection. The rest are still in hands of family members, most prominently attorney Ann Goodman, the great-granddaughter of C.M. and granddaughter of Kathryn. Ann was born well over a decade after C.M.'s passing so her recollections are not firsthand, but Kathryn is a different story. "She was extremely creative," Ann recalled, "a talented artist."

From her youth, Kathryn demonstrated a range of abilities. Around town, she was featured in performances, from recitations to piano recitals. Painting also served as an important form of expression. As a child, C.M. recognized his daughter's gift for recreating on canvas what she saw in real life. "He went out in the yard and just pulled up a vine and put it on the table and said, 'paint it,'" Ann remembered her grandmother saying, so she developed her painting skills. One cherished image depicts a child using a pumpkin as a paint bucket, dousing the leaves of a tree with fall colors, demonstrating how a child could change their own world through art.

While still a teenager, Kathryn competed with other high school students from across the state of North Carolina in a "declamation contest" held at then, Lenoir College. While others presented on current events of the day or the meaning of democracy, C.M. Hardin's daughter delivered a topic that would define her life. Her "Subject: The Photographer." With her father's help, she gained formal training in Chicago before returning to Hickory and joining her parents.

C.M. and Kathryn worked together for almost two decades. Although she learned from him, Kathryn never relayed much to her family about her professional relationship with her father. The only insights came through the pictures he took. "I know he did the school portraits because one of the photographs in my library is my grandmother and C.M. Hardin together in front of what is now the art museum because they were there to take school pictures," Ann points out, noting that for a long time the father/daughter combination were "virtually the only photographers" in Hickory,

After C.M. passed away in 1941, Kathryn took over the business with the help of her mother who continued her bookkeeping role for the family company. Over time, Kathryn concentrated on portrait and wedding photography. In 1954, she bought a house on the edge of town for a studio. The house still stands, though it now serves as the law office of Ann Goodman.

Ann never really considered a career as a photographer, though on occasion her grandmother tried to pass on techniques to the younger generation. Labeling her petite 'nanny' (she was 4'10") as a "sweet personality," Ann never developed an interest in photography like her grandmother. "Of all the talent that she had" Ann said, "she could not teach anybody, anything because it frustrated her." For example, "she was a beautiful seamstress and she was trying to help me learn to sew. It was so painful for her to watch. She would just snatch it out of your hands and do it herself."

Kathryn attempted to introduce her granddaughter to the mech-

-anics. of photography. The lessons were short. As Ann remembered, "She would corral me and get me in the dark room to try and teach me. But she did everything by feel. She just knew how long it took. She could see where the developing process was and know it was time to snatch it because it would keep developing. She would try to explain all this stuff. I'm standing in a dark room. I can't see what she was doing. She would get frustrated because she was explaining it. I was supposed to have that same feel. She just could not teach because it frustrated her."

A more intuitive assistant to Kathryn was her own daughter Peggy, Ann's mother. Much like her own mom, Peggy often helped out on both sides of the camera, as the business needed. She sat for more photographs than probably any person in town, but she also learned the business well enough to take over and close out the business in 1981 when Kathryn passed away. By that time, the photography studio was also serving as Ann's law office.

Located on 1st Avenue, the studio/office was remodeled in 1989 for the convenience of customers to the Goodman law firm, but many artifacts of the photography business remain. C.M.'s camera is still perched upon its heavy tripod, along with images of old Hickory lining the walls, a tribute to the painstaking work of the Hardin family. Much in the city has changed since C.M. first arrived with a picture-taking device in hand,

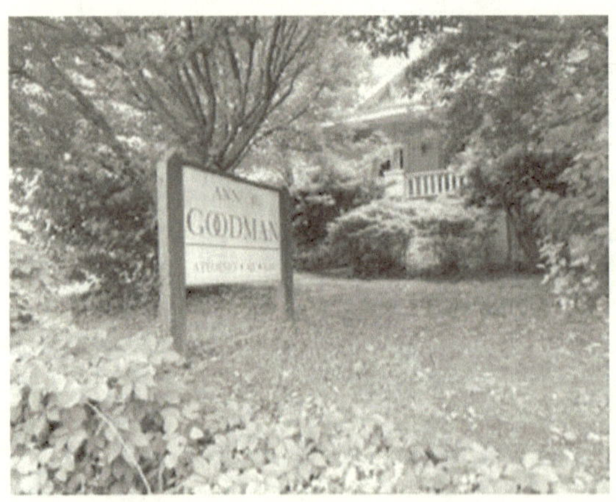

offering his services to document life in western North Carolina. The work of he and Kathryn served their time, but now, with each photo serving as a historical document, their work still enlightens.

ABOUT THE AUTHOR

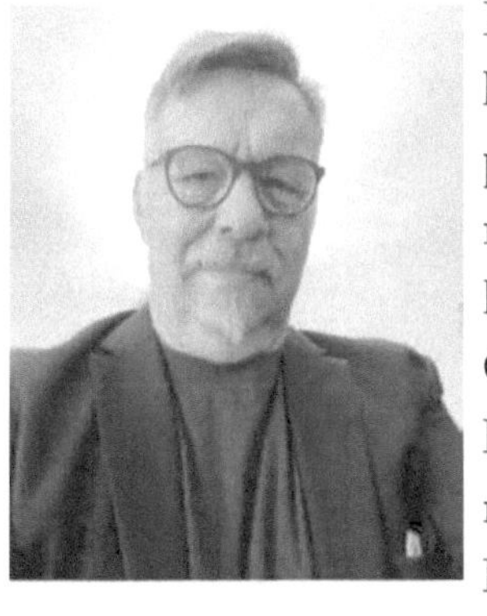

Richard Eller is the author of 14 historical books, celebrated for his ability to bring the past to life through vivid storytelling and meticulous research. He currently serves as a history professor at Catawba Valley Community College and is also the executive director of Redhawk Publications, where he champions regional voices and historical narratives. Richard lives in Hickory, North Carolina, with his wife, and is a proud and doting grandfather.

www.ingramcontent.com/pod-product-compliance
Lightning Source LLC
LaVergne TN
LVHW090534110826
845146LV00003B/1089
9798899330087